The Journey
for Justice

Sandra Rose Morris Kemp

ISBN 978-1-0980-2188-7 (paperback)
ISBN 978-1-0980-2189-4 (digital)

Christian Faith Publishing, Inc.
832 Park Avenue
Meadville, PA 16335
www.christianfaithpublishing.com

Printed in the United States of America

To the Morris-Kemp family

The Morris-Kemp Family

Top: Louise Kemp   Clara Morris
Middle: Christina Kemp   Sandra Kemp   Darryl Kemp
Bottom: Ivory Morris   Chauncey Kemp   Craig Kemp   Elmer Kemp

CONTENTS

ACKNOWLEDGMENT

My wholehearted gratitude goes to the following:

To God, for His inspiration and guidance
To my husband, for his support and encouragement to create the
    "story"
To my daughter, for computer and technical assistance
To the individuals who shared their oral histories
To repositories for providing resources
And to Christian Faith Publishing Inc. staff for making this story
    possible

INTRODUCTION

An African American Family's Contributions to the Struggle For Equality

On approaching my seventieth birthday, I felt it was time to write a book summarizing my fifty years of research about two communities and to bring closure to my experiences and challenges. The Belmead property was the plantation where my ancestors were enslaved. Mohemenco Hamlet (Macon District, Powhatan, Virginia) was the place where the Belmead freedmen settled during Reconstruction. These two communities are adjacent.

My goal is to preserve the history and heritage of these African Americans during the eras of slavery, reconstruction, segregation, and integration. Documents will show what was happening locally during these eras and how these ex-slaves and their descendants were involved in the struggle for equality and the contributions they made to this country as slaves and freed people, unsung heroes worthy of recognition.

I am saddened by two losses: The first loss is Belmead, which is to be sold soon. Belmead was first a plantation (Mount Pleasant) where enslaved African Americans were freed by Quaker slaveholders (Pleasant/Logan family) around 1800. Next, the Cocke family relocated slaves from Four Mile Tree, Mount Pleasant, and Swann's Point plantations in Surry County, Virginia, to Bremo (Fluvanna County, Virginia) and Belmead/Beldale (Powhatan County, Virginia).

Initially, white tradesmen were used as builders. Later, enslaved individuals were trained in the building occupations. The slaves were given religious principles. Most enslaved families were kept together. After slavery, the ex-slaves labored as sharecroppers on the property.

In the late 1800s, the Drexel/Morrell family (Pennsylvania) established boarding schools for African American and Native American boys and girls on the property. Very few of the students were from the local community in Powhatan. The parents of the local students could not afford the tuition. Scholarships were not offered to them. Those who attended the schools came from various states in this country. Most were African Americans. My ancestors were enslaved on these plantations and were employed at these schools. The schools were places for education, employment, religion, and recreational/cultural activities. My family has been associated with Belmead property for over 180 years. My enslaved ancestors left us a "legacy of Belmead ties."

The biography of my great-grandfather James Morris tells the history of James Morris's children, grandchildren, and great-grandchildren and their association with the Belmead Plantation, Belmead Farm, and the three schools on Belmead property.

The second loss is Mohemenco community (hamlet). History records that Mohemenco was one of two Monacan (Siouan) Native American villages in Powhatan. Mohemenco is in transition. I hold twelve acres of land in this community. I was born in Richmond, Virginia, at Saint Phillip's Hospital for Colored (now part of the Virginia Commonwealth University (VCU)/Medical College of Virginia (MCV). Fifteen years later (1961), my youngest sister would be recovering from Reye's syndrome–like symptoms at the same hospital. I spent the first eighteen years of my life in Mohemenco. In 1963, I became one of sixty-five infants (legal term) to integrate the Powhatan County Public Schools and the first African American graduate in 1965. After high school, I enrolled in the VCU School of Arts and received a bachelor's degree in fine arts, majoring in fashion design. I was the first African American to graduate from the fashion design program in 1971. Thereafter, I moved North and West to pursue higher education and career advancement.

In 1988, I returned to the metropolitan Richmond area/ Mohemenco. The changes in Mohemenco startled me! The following are a few of the changes: family names such as *Hazel, Carrington*, and *Wood* have disappeared; a local church Sunday school's membership for youth has dropped from fifty plus to five or less; and the community is still designated as agriculture, but the African American history, heritage, and culture are being obliterated! Mohemenco was the place where ex-slaves purchased land tracts that were parts of plantations that no longer were profitable without slave labor. After the Civil War, during Reconstruction, and later, these freedmen farmed, built homes, churches/cemeteries, and schools. Some of the ex-slaves and their descendants worked at Belmead schools as instructors, tradesmen, agricultural workers, maintenance staff, and domestics. Many left the community temporarily. They went North for economic reasons but returned to their land after short stays or after retirement. Mohemenco was a place that instilled values that allowed the ex-slaves' descendants to become self-actualized and productive members of society.

The demise of the Belmead property and the transformation of the Mohemenco community have spurred me to educate the family, community, county, state, country, and world by recording the histories that will disappear forever, as we know them, if not documented to preserve the African American history/heritage piece, lest we forget. I wish to prevent the African Americans' tremendous contributions to this country from being deleted from history and dispel the images of African Americans as criminals and the causes of the country's problems. The history tells the story of African Americans during slavery, reconstruction, segregation, and integration periods.

CHAPTER 1

The Cocke, Faulcon, Browne, and Bowdoin Families of Surry County, Virginia, and the Enslaved African Americans on the Plantations

The first Cocke to arrive in Virginia was Richard Cocke. He was a prominent colonial Virginia planter and politician. Among his more prominent descendants are General Robert E. Lee and US presidents George Washington, Thomas Jefferson, George H. W. Bush, and George W. Bush.

Richard Cocke was born in 1597 at Pickthorn, Stottesdon, Shropshire, England. He was the son of Thomas Cocke, a yeoman farmer. The first Virginia record of Cocke was December 24, 1627, when he appeared at the court in Jamestown to give testimony as the purser of the Thomas and John that four men of Mr. Sharples had run away while being transported to Virginia. On June 5, 1632, Cocke married Temperance Bailey, the widow of John Browne. Temperance was born about 1617 in Virginia. She was the daughter of Thomas Bailey and Cicely Jordan Farrar, who had arrived in Virginia in 1610.

Temperance had children by John Browne. Richard Cocke and Temperance had two sons, Thomas and Richard (the elder). Richard, following the death of Temperance, married Mary Aston, a daughter of Walter Aston, and had the following children: another son Richard (the younger), Elizabeth, John, William, and Edward.

By the time Cocke died in 1665, he owned 10,916 acres of land spread over three sites in Henrico—Bremo, Malvern Hill, and Curles. He also owned land in Surry County, Virginia, in the early 1630s. Four of his descendants were Richard Cocke VI, John Hartwell Cocke II, Sally (Cocke) Faulcon, and Philip St. George Cocke. Richard the sixth was the brother of John Hartwell Cocke I. He served as the guardian of John Hartwell Cocke II and resided at Mount Pleasant Plantation, which John Hartwell II inherited upon reaching the age of majority. Richard the sixth freed his slaves in his will. Richard's niece Sally (Cocke) Faulcon, sister to John Hartwell II, was married to Nicholas Faulcon. They purchased Mount Pleasant Plantation from Sally's brother John in 1809. In her will, she offered freedom to any slave that chose to leave Virginia and go to Africa. Around the time of the sale of the Surry property and the Buckingham property (Bear Garden), John moved to Fluvanna County, Virginia, to Bremo Plantations (upper, lower, and recess). John sent a number of his slaves to Liberia, West Africa, as a member of the American Colonization Society. Later he sent a number of his slaves to his cotton plantation in Alabama in preparation for freedom and emigration to Liberia.

Philip St. George Cocke, John's son, married Sally Elizabeth Courtney Bowdoin, the granddaughter of William Browne Jr. Her parents were Sally Browne and John Tucker Bowdoin. William Browne owned Four Mile Tree Plantation. In his will of 1799, he left his slaves to his daughter Sally Bowdoin, and they were to be freed at her death. She died in 1815, giving her slaves their freedom, and the Four Mile Tree Plantation went to her husband, John Tucker Bowdoin. Upon his death, Sally Bowdoin and Philip Cocke inherited the plantation and the property in Brunswick County, Virginia: Arthur Creek (1,390 acres and 30 slaves), Rose Creek (1,762 acres and 24 slaves), Meherrin (2,059 acres and 64 slaves), and Pea Hill (1,200 acres and 43 slaves). Rose Creek became the location of the African American St. Paul's College in Lawrenceville, Virginia, after slavery.

During slavery, Rose Creek was a supply station for the breeding and training of slaves. The general made his headquarters at Meherrin, where he had a fortress-looking stone house situated on an elevation overlooking the Meherrin River and surrounded by what in the distance seems to be the stone houses of the retainers, suggesting a feudal castle of the old days. Rose Creek and Peas Hill had substantial log houses for the overseers and mud and dirt houses for the slaves, some single and some double. These houses preserved traditions of the ancestral homes of the Negro in Africa, both in appearance and in materials. Board frames were first put up in the size of the intended house. The mud was moistened, worked to the proper consistency, and mixed with straw to secure adhesives, and then poured and rammed into the chamber between the boards. The walls were allowed to dry, and the top, usually clapboards or shingles of heart pine, put on. Great care had to be taken to protect the walls at the point of structure with the roof from dripping water, which if allowed to seep through, would soften them and soon cause decay. After the walls had hardened sufficiently, the enclosing boards were removed. In most cases, the mud walls were kept whitewashed; and in the course of time, the huts took on the appearance of a beautiful white stone structure, the illusion being most effective on moonlit nights.

Later Philip Cocke sold the Surry County and Brunswick plantations and sent the slaves to his Mississippi cotton plantations (five). He built his Belmead mansion in Powhatan County, Virginia. [1]

John Hartwell Cocke II (1780–1866)

John Hartwell Cocke II (1780–1866) was born on Mount Pleasant Plantation in Surry County, Virginia. His parents were John Hartwell Cocke I and Elizabeth Kennon Cocke. He was one of eight children. His father owned three large plantations and 130 slaves. He

---

[1] "Richard Cocke," *Wikipedia*, https: en.wikipedia.org/wiki/Richard Cocke/.
"Cox Family Story, General Cox," AncientFaces.com.

SANDRA ROSE MORRIS KEMP

was orphaned by the age of twelve. He inherited his father's Mount Pleasant Plantation and slaves, which he took over after coming of age. He attended the College of William & Mary, graduating in 1798.

Cocke married Anne Barraud in Norfolk in 1802. He renovated the plantation home in Surry County. In 1809, Cocke sold the plantation to his sister Sally and her husband, Nicholas Faulcon (a native of Surry County, born in 1773, and the son of Nicholas Faulcon Sr. and his wife, Lucy Wyatt). Faulcon served as a delegate to the General Assembly (1799–1803) and represented Surry, Isle of Wight, and Prince George Counties in the state Senate. His father served in the House of Burgesses and represented Surry County during the conventions held during the Revolutionary War. Cocke moved his family to Bremo Plantation (3,100 acres). The property was divided into three sections: lower, upper, and recess. The tract was located on the northern bank of the James River in Fluvanna County in the piedmont. He worked out new methods of scientific farming and helped to found the Agricultural Society of Fluvanna County. He served as justice of the peace. During the War of 1812, Cocke was commissioned as a brigadier general in command of the Virginia militia based out of Camp Carter and Camp Holly. His brigade was composed of companies of troops from Fluvanna County.

After the war, Cocke returned to his estate at Bremo and, in 1819, completed construction of a large plantation mansion at Upper Bremo with the master builder John Neilson, who had worked with Thomas Jefferson on Monticello. In 1819, Cocke was appointed by Virginia Governor James Patton Preston to the first Board of Visitors of the University of Virginia. He served until 1852. The General Assembly selected him in 1823 to the State Board of Public Works. In 1835, Cocke joined the board of directors of the James River and Kanawha Company, which was established to develop canals to improve water transportation along two hundred miles of the James River. However, he opposed their decision in 1838 to allow liquor to its laborers. He erected a Greek revival temple over a spring along the canal at Bremo to encourage bargemen to consume water. He organized an anti-liquor society for local blacks, including his own slaves.

Cocke suspected that one slave, Tom Drew, had returned to the use of alcohol. In 1856, he was condemning the use of wine in communion services as a desecration of the sacrament. He participated in the Virginia Society for the Promotion of Temperance (also known as the Temperance Society of Virginia) from 1826 to 1834. He was active in the American Temperance Society (American Temperance Union) from 1836 to 1843.

Cocke participated in several efforts to reform different aspects of society, including temperance and gradual emancipation of slaves. He served as president of the state and national temperance unions. He inherited a number of slaves. He promoted using "education and skill training" to prepare slaves for freedom and colonization in Africa. One neighbor (pro-slaver) violently attacked Cocke. Some equated John Hartwell to sheep sorrel. By 1848, Cocke started a second plantation in Alabama as a place for slaves to prepare to live independently, as free people in the colony of Liberia. He supported them with supplies and books and spent his own money to send these slaves to the colony. Cocke promoted the American Society for Colonizing the Free People of Color of the United States (known as the American Colonization Society [ACS]) in 1825.

He declared that the physical deterioration of people who used tobacco was an affront to God. He circulated these tracts and distributed medal to boys who promised never to use the weed. Cocke fought against the cultivation and use of tobacco, one of Virginia's agricultural staples. Cocke inherited several large tobacco plantations. He continued to grow the crop until 1840, when for economic and moral reasons, he ceased planting tobacco. He detailed his objections in a pamphlet, *Tobacco, the Bane of Virginia Husbandry* (1860). He asserted that Virginia could not prosper as long as planters remained entranced by a crop that exhausted the land and diverted labor and time from the production of food and clothing. In 1860, he owned 135 bondsmen in Alabama and Virginia.

Even though he owned slaves, initially he thought slavery to be against God's will and argued that removing African Americans to Africa was the best solution to the institution's various evils. He believed that his slaves possessed immortal souls and natural rights and had been rendered unfit for liberty only by "the debasing influence of their bondage." He considered it his responsibility to educate, evangelize, and deport them. Cocke's opposition to abolitionism and his support of the Confederacy during the American Civil War caused his views to become pro-slavery over time. He reevaluated his opinion of slavery during the 1860s (partly due to the failure of his Alabama experiment and his belief that the abolitionists had forced the nation into war) and concluded that slavery was "of Divine Origin" and that God intended blacks to remain enslaved. During the war, Cocke served as a captain in the artillery in 1860. After the war, Cocke applied for a presidential pardon due to his wealth and took the amnesty oath on August 1, 1865. He died on June 24, 1866, and was buried in the family plot at Bremo Plantation in Bremo Bluff, Fluvanna County, Virginia.[2]

Histories of Mount Pleasant and Bremo Plantations

Mount Pleasant was first settled by the English in 1620 as a plantation called Pace's Paines and was continuously inhabited. In the seventeenth century, the property was controlled by the Swann family. Throughout most of the eighteenth century, it belonged to the Cocke family, notably John Hartwell Cocke, the builder of Bremo. In 1709, John Hartwell acquired the 1,650-acre Swann's Point Plantation, which included Mount Pleasant. The tract eventually fell to Richard Cocke IV around 1730 when he married Hartwell's daughter and heir, Elizabeth. Around 1750, they built the present dwelling, and later it was named Mount Pleasant. The chronological history of the land and people of Mount Pleasant include the following: Richard Pace, Frances Chapman, William Perry, William Swann, Thomas Swann, Samuel Swann, Joseph Jack Jackman, George Marable II,

---

[2.] "John Hartwell Cocke," *Wikipedia*, https://en.wikipedia.org/wiki/John Hartwell Cocke.
"Cocke, John Hartwell (1780–1866)," http://www.encyclopediavirginia.org/ Cocke John Hartwell 1780-1866.

John Hartwell, Richard (IV) and Elizabeth Hartwell Cocke, Hartwell Cocke I, John Hartwell Cocke I, John Hartwell Cocke II, Nicholas and Sally Cocke Faulcon, and George Wilson.[3]

Bremo Plantation is an estate covering 1,500 acres on the west side of Bremo Bluff in Fluvanna County, Virginia. The large mansion at Upper Bremo was designed by owner John Hartwell Cocke in consultation with John Neilson (b. 1770–1827). The estate includes two smaller residences built at Lower Bremo and Bremo Recess. The plantation overlooks the James River. Bremo is a well-preserved example of Jeffersonian architecture.

James Moss, white artisan, was employed at Bremo Recess from 1802 to 1818. He built the granary, tobacco house, stable, icehouse, carpentry shop, laundry, smokehouse, kitchen, dairy, and weaving house. Thomas Whitelaw constructed the stone range with the labor of Cato (African American) and the stone barn. Originally, white artisans did the construction; later his Negroes were trained as masons, carpenters, and bricklayers. Blacks also served as overseers: Champion at Bremo Recess (1806 to 1808 and 1814); Jessie at Upper Bremo (1821); and George at Upper Bremo (1830–1831) and Lower Bremo (1832–1834). To operate an efficient and financially successful plantation, owners employed slave labor, hired out slaves, and sold slaves to generate income or rid the plantation of troublemakers. If possible, the slaves were sold along with family members to members of the owner's family in an effort to keep the slave family together. At times, this was not possible, and the slave was sold and separated from his family.

Starting in 1808, Cocke built an estate of three houses along the James River, which he named *Bremo* after his family's ancestral home of Braemore in Scotland. One of the original structures was an ancestral hunting lodge at Lower Bremo that was built of stone and dated back to 1725. Cocke inhabited this lodge close to the river as his first home on the estate. Around 1812, Cocke completed a larger home for his family at Bremo Recess, situated on higher ground far-

---

[3.] "Mount Pleasant Plantation," http://mountpleasantplantation.com/.

ther back from the James River. This house incorporated elements of Jacobean architecture.

During his time at Lower Bremo and Bremo Recess, Cocke worked on the designing of a grand plantation mansion to be built at Upper Bremo. He utilized hand-molded brick. It took several years and was completed in 1819. The neighboring barn was adorned with columns. During slavery, Cocke had built a chapel for his slaves on the plantation. Later in 1881, John's son and others purchased land in Bremo Bluff and relocated it. The chapel was consecrated as part of an Episcopal church.[4]

Philip St. George Cocke (1809–1861)

Philip Cocke was born at Bremo Bluff in Fluvanna County, Virginia (some resources list Surry County, Virginia, as his place of birth). He was the son of John Hartwell Cocke II and his first wife, Anne Barraud Cocke. He attended the University of Virginia before entering the United States Military Academy at West Point, New York, in 1828. After graduating sixth in a class of forty-four in 1832, he served as a second lieutenant of artillery in the United States Army and was stationed at Charleston, South Carolina, during the Nullification Crisis. He served from 1832 to 1833 and became adjutant of the Second United States Artillery. In 1834, he resigned his commission and became a planter in Powhatan, Virginia, and purchased land in Mississippi for cotton plantations. In the same year, he married Sally Elizabeth Courtney Bowdoin in Surry County, Virginia. They had eleven children.

In 1835, he commissioned architect A. J. Davis to build a manor house named *Belmead*. Cocke was a wealthy plantation owner who accumulated hundreds of slaves (610) and owned 27,000 acres of land. Cocke became an accomplished agriculturalist, publishing articles in journals, as well as a book on plantation management

---

[4.] Bremo Historic District, *Wikipedia*, https://en.wikipedia.org/wiki/Bremo Historic District.

entitled *Plantation and Farm Instruction* (1854). He was president of the Virginia State Agricultural Society. In 1859, he organized a militia infantry company known as the Powhatan Troop in response to the John Brown's raid on Harpers Ferry to help defend Powhatan County in case of a similar action or slave revolt in the future.

When volunteers were combined into the Confederate Army following the start of the American Civil War (1861–1865), Cocke's rank was reduced from brigadier general to colonel. He took offense and later complained when Confederate General Pierre G. T. Beauregard did not praise him enough during the First Battle of Manassas. In a state of despondency and mental anguish over what he regarded as poor treatment by General Robert E. Lee and others, he shot himself in the head on December 26, 1861, at his mansion, Belmead, in Powhatan County, Virginia. He was initially buried on the plantation grounds, but he was reinterred in 1904 at Hollywood Cemetery, Richmond, Virginia. The plantation was put up for sale after the war ended.[5]

Histories of Four-Mile Tree and Belmead/Beldale Plantations

Four-Mile Tree was a plantation near Jamestown, Virginia, composed of two thousand acres. It was on the south bank of the James River opposite Jamestown, four miles farther north. It overlooked the James River. This was the seat of the Browne Family for two hundred years, during the reign of Charles I until the death of the last male heir (William Browne) in 1799. The first owner, Colonel Henry Browne, was a member of Sir William Berkley's council in 1643. The plantation house was constructed around 1745. Its grave site contains the oldest legible tombstone in Virginia.

The plantation, named for its distance from Jamestown, was one of Surry's more prosperous, producing tobacco with slaves from

---

[5.] "Cocke, Philip St. George (1809–1861)," http://www.encyclopediavirginia. org/Cocke Philip St George 1809-1861.

an early period. The Brownes were justices of the County Court throughout the colonial period. Several members of the family served on the governor's council or in the House of Burgesses during the seventeenth century. During the War for Independence, William Browne was a member of the Surry Committee of Safety and lieutenant colonel of militia. His son was a lieutenant in the revolutionary militia. The British sacked the plantation during the War of 1812.

John Tucker Bowdoin married Sally Edwards Browne, daughter of William Browne of Four Mile Tree plantation. She died on November 26, 1815 leaving a daughter, Sally Elizabeth Courtney Bowdoin (b. May 6, 1815). Browne's slaves were freed upon her death. Bowdoin traveled a great deal and had medical problems. He died in 1821. Bowdoin left his estate to his daughter. The estate included Four Mile Tree plantation and plantations in Brunswick County, Virginia. Sally E. C. Bowdoin lived with Nicholas and Sally Cocke Faulcon. Nicholas Faulcon and John Hartwell Cocke were her legal guardians. Nicholas Faulcon, John Cocke, and John Faulcon were the executors for the estate. John T. Bowdoin was buried at Four Mile Tree. Philip and Sally lived at Four Mile Tree until 1840. Later, Philip St. George Cocke sold the Four Mile Tree plantation and the property in Brunswick County that his wife had inherited and moved his family to another plantation, Belmead, in Powhatan County, Virginia, and purchased property in Mississippi for the production of cotton: Malvern (1,552 acres and 93 slaves), Malvern Hill (1,552 acres and 73 slaves), Malvern Lake (1,552 acres and 36 slaves), Silver Creek (2,000 acres and 42 slaves), and Yazoo River (788 acres and 42 slaves).[6]

Belmead Plantation is a historic home located in Powhatan County, Virginia, that was purchased by Philip Cocke in 1838. The house is a two-story stuccoed Gothic Revival–style brick residence with a three-story central cross gable. It features a square tower with corner piers, crenelation, belt courses, ground level Tudor-arched

---

[6.] "Four Mile Tree," *Wikipedia*, https://en.wikipedia.org/wiki/Four Mile Tree.

openings, and diamond-paned casement windows. The roofline has clusters of circular and polygonal shaped chimney stacks and stepped gable ends. It was designed by architect Alexander Jackson Davis and constructed about 1845. Approximately 150 slaves worked the land, growing tobacco and grains. Belmead was composed of 2,306 acres, and the adjacent Beldale tract contained 2,197 acres with 36 slaves.

Cocke admired Gothic architecture and sponsored the New York architect who worked in that style. Under Cocke's patronage, Davis designed Belmead and Emmanuel Episcopal Church in Powhatan, where Cocke and his family worshipped, as well as Gothic Revival structures for the Virginia Military Institute. Cocke also engaged Davis to prepare a Greek Revival design for the Powhatan County Courthouse.

In 1879, the property was conveyed to the Sisters of the Blessed Sacrament for Indians and Colored People and opened as St. Emma's Industrial and Agricultural School for African American Children. St Emma's Military Academy for boys and St. Francis de Sales for girls are credited with educating fifteen thousand black students. The schools closed in the early 1970s. In 2016, the order of the Sisters of the Blessed Sacrament, headquartered in Philadelphia, Pennsylvania, put the 2,265 acres known as Belmead Plantation on the market for sale.

The original tract, Belle Meade, has had a number of owners (Quakers, Episcopalians, and Catholics) since 1715 to the present: Bartholomew Stovall, George Stovall, John Pleasants, Dr. Charles Logan and Mary Pleasants Logan, Mary (Pleasants) Logan and Robert Cary Pleasants, Thomas Bolling Tabb, Dr. Michael K. Murray, and Thomas Bolling Tabb's widow. In 1800, in the case of *Pleasants v. Pleasants*, a number of slaves had been freed by a Quaker in his will. The will was not honored, and the court finally freed the so-named slaves in the will on Belle Meade.

In 1838, Philip Cocke purchased 1,170 acres from Tabb's widow and 182 acres (Mount Erin) from M. K. Murray. In 1845, he purchased 553 acres from George Tinsley and his wife. In 1845, he purchased Dunlora/Deep Creek Estate/Beldale from Pleasant and Sarah Finch. Dunlora was a plantation owned by Ms. Ann Hickman.

The Virginia Baptist Education Society established in 1830 a school for ministers at Dunlora. This school was known locally as Dunlora Academy. Reverend Edward Baptist, principal, resigned in 1832, and the school was moved to Henrico County and then to Richmond. From it developed Richmond College and, later, the University of Richmond. Fonthill was purchased from General Mosby's estate. The Cocke family owned the land as a plantation/farm for fifty-one years (1838 to 1889); Philip for twenty-three years; Sally (Mrs. Philip Cocke) for eleven years; and John Bowdoin Cocke (Philip's eldest son) for seventeen years.

In 1889 Edward Hannewinckel bought Belmead after John's death and John's wife (Betty) and their 3 daughters moved to Charlottesville, Virginia.

In 1893, Colonel Edward and Louise Morrell bought Belmead (1,640 acres) from Hannewinckel and Mount Erin (630 acres) from J. C. and Sarah Bowles. Mount Erin was deeded to Sr. Katherine Drexel of the Sisters of the Blessed Sacrament by the Morrells. The Morrell/Drexel family owned this tract for seventy-seven years as schools (1893–1970s). Mrs. Morrell gave the title to Belmead to the Board of Trustees. Ms. A. L. Colby, last trustee, gave the deed for Belmead to the Sisters of the Blessed Sacrament.[7]

[7.] "Belmead (Powhatan, Virginia)," *Wikipedia*, https://en.wikipedia.org/wiki/Belmead, (Powhatan Virginia).
Various Stories and Misc. Info Relating to Belmead, assembled bv Sr. Marian McDonald (June 16, 2002).
"Plantation and Farm Instruction (1854)," Philip St. George Cocke, Virginia Historical Society.
Report on Deaths on Belmead Plantation, Powhatan County, Virginia (1853–1865), clerk's office.

CHAPTER 2

Looking for Rebecca[8]

My great-great grandmother Rebecca was a slave associated with the Swann's Point/Mount Pleasant and Four Mile Tree Plantations in Surry County, Virginia. She was the mother of James Morris, Alfred Morris, and Melvina (Jones) Taylor. Two other siblings, Philemon and Freeman, whereabouts are lost to history for now. They were born in Surry County, Virginia, but later came to Philip St. George

---

[8.] University of Virginia Small Special Collection, Cocke Manuscripts 640 Box 1, Inventories.
"Historical Background of Mt. Pleasant," Mount Pleasant Plantation, http://mountpleasantplantation.com/?page id=114.
"Virginia Slaves Freed in Virginia After 1782," Surry County will abstracts, http://www.freeafricansamericans.com.virginiafreeafter1782.htm.

Randall M. Miller, ed., *Dear Master: Letters of a Slave Family* (The University of Georgia Press).
Dennis Hudgins, "Surry County Virginia Register of Free Negroes," Virginia Genealogical Society.
Roll of Emigrants that have been sent to the colony of Liberia, Western Africa, by the America, http://ccharity.com/liberia/index.htm.

Virginia Historical Society, Plantation and Farm Instruction (1854), Philip St. George Cocke.
1853-1865 Report of Deaths on Belmead Plantation, Powhatan County, Virginia Clerk's Office.
Powhatan County, Virginia Register of Deaths.

Cocke's Belmead and Beldale Plantations. James (b. 1820) was a carpenter and miller. Alfred (b. 1816) was a stonemason. After slavery, he became a minister of the Gospel. Their sister Melvina (b. 1837) was a field hand. She married Charleston Taylor, a carpenter on the plantation. As the informant for Melvina's death certificate, he stated that her parents were Jeff and Rebecca Jones, and Melvina was born in Surry. To try to locate "Rebecca" and "Jeff," I reviewed the inventories of the Surry plantations, Powhatan plantations, and Fluvanna plantations of the Cocke Family.

On a 1771 inventory of Mount Pleasant/Swann's Point Plantation for John Hartwell Cocke I, a "Beck" (?) (b. 1765) is listed among thirty-three slaves. In a 1782 inventory of the Surry Plantation for John Hartwell Cocke II (Richard Cocke VI serving as executor), a "Beck" and four children are listed; and in 1788, there is a "Becky" (adult) and a "Beck" (under sixteen years of age). In 1791, a "Becky Short" (?) (b. 1765) is listed as property of John Hartwell II. In 1800, Richard Cocke VI asks his nephew to free Becky and her son Robert Kennon (b. 1795) in his will. Later, Becky Short's two other sons William Short (b. 1808) and Richard Short (b. 1811) are listed as free on the Surry County Register of African American by way of Richard's will. This is probably not my Rebecca. She was past reproductive years in the period of 1816–1837 when Alfred, James, and Melvina were born. Since she was freed, her children would have been freed. My aforementioned ancestors were enslaved until emancipation and the Civil War. The slave count on this plantation was forty-four in 1791. In reviewing the records, the names of Moses Short and Peyton Short appear.

In 1826, Nicholas Faulcon of Mount Pleasant Plantation left his wife, Sally (Cocke) Faulcon, *life rights* in twenty-five slaves. The following have familiar ties: old Hailey; James Hailey and wife, Betsy, and daughter Betsy; Alfred; and Dianna and her children Evelyn, Cornelius, Scipio, and "Beck." James had a brother named Alfred, and James named one of his sons Hailey (listed as a child on the Belmead Plantation inventory). Perhaps this is the connection to the Surry Plantation of Mount Pleasant.

In the twenty-eight slaves that Nicholas left Sally outright ownership, several had the last name of *Jones*: Liza Jones and her three children and Peter Jones.

William Browne of Four Mile Tree in his will of 1799 freed Mary Anne Jones on the death of Sally Edwards (Browne) Bowdoin in 1815.

In the 1800 inventory of Richard VI, the names of Cesar Jones and Paul Jones appear.

The Belmead/Beldale records contain information relating to the enslaved Morris (also referred to as Morse or Moss) family.

The 1854, 1861, and 1863 inventories and death reports were reviewed for the African American family named *Morris*. The following information was found:

- "Jeffry" (b. 1801)
- "James" (b. 1823), carpenter and miller
- "Alfred Mor——" (b. 1816), stonemason
- "Priscilla" (b. 1823, Surry, Virginia), housemaid/field hand, died 1857

Children/parents

Priscilla and James were parents to the following children:

- "Kitty" (b. 1849)
- "Irena" (b. 1849)
- "Tucker" (b. 1852, d. 1857)
- "Mahala" (b. 1853)
- "Hailey" (b. 1853)
- "Nelly" (b. 1855, d. 1855)

Other references to "Becky," "Becca," or "Rebecca"

- "Becky" appears on the 1853–1865 death report
- "Thomas" (b. 1829, d. 1854) age twenty-five, mother "Becky"

- "Becky" (b. 1850), age thirteen, Beldale Plantation
- Martha (b. 1841), daughter of "Becky"

There were 126 slaves on Belmead Plantation and 37 on Beldale Plantation.

African Americans on the Bremo Plantations with the surnames of "Morris," "Morse," or "Moss"

- Morse Jones
- Albert
- Albert Jr.
- Ann
- Betsey
- Cain
- Carter
- (?) old Champion, first foreman at Lower Bremo
- Champion[9]
- Charles
- Jinny
- Kessiah
- Martha
- Matilda
- Matthew
- Rebecca, Becky or Becca Bird[10]
- Sandy

[9.] Champion Morris (b. 1810) was married three times. The following are his wives:
Jane (died in 1845),
Becky Bird (with whom he had two children), and Emma.

[10.] Champion left Becky after 1865. Letters from the Skipwith family in Liberia to General Cocke indicate that Becky was alive as late as 1856. Champion Morris was the son of Harry Morse and Ann "Sucky" Faulcon (sister of Daphne Faulcon, who married Tom Drew). My Becky should have been born around 1796. The date of Becky Bird's birth is questionable. This Rebecca comes close to the Jones-Morris tie. She could possibly be the Rebecca that I have been looking to find.

Surnames of Some of the Enslaved African Americans

The nineteen plantations of the Cocke family are the following: Mount Pleasant/Swann's Point and Four-Mile Tree Plantations (Surry County, Virginia); Belmead and Bedale Plantations (Powhatan County, Virginia); Bremo (Upper, Lower, and Recess) Plantations (Fluvanna County, Virginia); Bear Garden Plantation (Buckingham County, Virginia); Arthur Creek, Rose Creek, Meherrin, and Pea Hill Plantations (Brunswick County, Virginia); New Hope and Hopewell Plantations (Alabama); and five plantations in Mississippi. The surname of some of the enslaved African Americans on the plantations include the following:

- Benedict
- Brown
- Buckner
- Blackburn
- Bolling
- Bird
- Byrd
- Bentley
- Benson
- Cooper
- Cannon
- Culpepper
- Cocke
- Chambers
- Creasy
- Cox
- Clayton
- Drew
- Dabney
- Edwards
- Faulcon
- Frazer
- Griffin
- Gault
- Green
- Haskin
- Hailey
- Howell
- Harris
- Hewitt
- Jones
- Johnson
- James
- Kennon
- Keller
- Low

However, her two sons and daughter are documented as being on the Belmead Plantation through multiple documents that will be presented under the section "James Morris Biography."

- Lewis
- Logan
- Lomax
- Lynch
- Morse/Morris/Moss
- McGill
- Nicholas
- Pryor
- Randall
- Richards
- Sturdivant (Studvent, Stuvant, Sturtevant, Stupin)
- Skipwith
- Short
- Simms
- Smith
- Story
- Scott
- Turner
- Trent
- Taylor
- Tyler
- Travis
- Thomas
- Tompkin
- Tucker
- Woodley
- Washington

CHAPTER 3

Virginia Slave Laws and Codes

Slavery on *Wikipedia* is defined as "any system in which principles of property law applies to people, allowing individuals to own, buy, and sell other individuals as a de jure form of property." A slave is unable to withdraw unilaterally from such an arrangement and works without remuneration. The term *chattel slavery* is used to refer to this specific sense of legalized de jure slavery. The word *slavery* may also refer to any situation in which an individual is forced to work against their own will—unfree labor or forced labor.

These Virginia Laws (judicial ruling and statute) and the Constitution totaling 131 began in 1630 and continued to 1872. Blacks were enslaved for life and considered property. These codes related to miscegenation, firearms, duty, runaways, children, slavery legalization, penal code, free blacks, slave codes, racial status, freedom of movement, manumission, property rights, military service, commerce, slave status, slave trade, anti-emancipation, ownership, free blacks, transporting the enslaved, rebellion, commerce, kidnapping, hiring out, registry of enslaved/free blacks, unlawful assembly, education, emancipation, certification, alcohol, patrols, insanity, re-enslavement, gaming, property, drugs, voluntary re-inslavement, enslavement outlawed, and children of the enslaved.[11]

[11.] "Slavery in America, Virginia Slave Law Summary and Record," http://www.slaveryinamerica.org/geography/slave laws VA.htm.

The laws and codes left the enslaved African Americans scarred and dehumanized. The codes relating to plantation rules, runaway slaves, manumission, miscegenation, and education are defined and described as they relate to the enslaved African Americans on the Surry County, Virginia, plantations (3); the Powhatan County, Virginia, plantations (2); the Fluvanna County, Virginia, plantations (3); the Brunswick County, Virginia, plantations (4); and the Buckingham County, Virginia, plantation (1) of the Browne-Bowdoin and Cocke-Faulcon families.

1. Plantation Slave Codes, 1792 Statute

This code contained fifty-three acts that covered the importation of blacks, freedom of movement among those enslaved, prohibitions against bearing arms, punishments for rebellious behavior, unlawful assembly, trading with blacks, attacks on whites by a black, punishment for attempted rape of a white woman (castration), procedures for capturing runaways, prohibitions against enslaved blacks administering medicines, legal counsel for blacks accused of criminal offenses, perjury punishable by cutting off the offender's ears plus thirty-nine lashes, provisions for emancipation, and prohibited shipmaster from transporting enslaved persons out of state without master's consent. The Code also defined a mulatto as a person with one quarter black blood.

The plantation and farm instruction regulation record of Philip St. George Cocke of Belmead, Powhatan County, Virginia, Inventory and Account Book (1854) contains the plantation management rules on obedience, resistance/arrest, spirits, stealing, lying, adultery, fornication, profanity, fighting, quarreling, written pass, selling, visiting, marrying, running about at night, cleanliness, punishment, giving evidence against others, reading of the rules, assembling for work, sick reporting, animal care, illness care, meal time and diet requirements, inspection of quarters and dress, quarter accommodations, clothing, weekly food provisions, making of fiber production for making clothing, vegetable/kitchen gardens, retire to rest and manager inspections, and night patrol parties. The Record also included slave inventories, daily weather information, and work schedules.

General John Hartwell Cocke of Bremo encountered problems in making the transition between slavery and free labor—contracts and treatment of his employees. A government official was present, who approved of the transaction when Cocke contracted with his Negroes in September 1865 for labor at wage rates instead of requiring from them a blanket submission to his old rules. In 1866, Cocke's son drew up a number of contracts for his laborers to sign. He specified that they were to be paid out of the proceeds of farm crops—beginning of the transition to sharecropping. Some of the Negroes left their former master's employ. Freedman Benjamin Creasy addressed a letter to Cocke wishing him well and agreeing to put in another year.

Creasy left the plantation. John Bowdoin Cocke at Belmead drew up a labor contract for his Negroes. He and his mother, Courtney Cocke, wrote letters to John Hartwell Cocke complaining about the departure of many of their former slaves. John also complained about one ex-slave who had walked from Belmead to Bremo and, after emancipation, requested a mule to ride instead of walking.

In a letter dated July 27, 1865, an officer of the Freedmen's Bureau (Captain Frank P. Crandon) in Gordonsville wrote the following to Cocke:

> I am informed that you have been in the habit of whipping negroes on your plantation. This is in violation of Military orders in force in this district. You will abstain from doing this... This man says he has been at work for you. He says further that you threatened to give him nine and thirty lashes for some offence... I do not know that you have so threatened, but you will see the necessity of not punishing any hands upon your place in this way.[12]

[12.] Virginia Historical Society, Belmead Farm Books.
Coyner Jr., Martin Boyd, "John Hartwell Cocke of Bremo: Agriculture and Slavery in the Antebellum South," doctoral dissertation (University of Virginia, 1961).

2. Run Away Slaves Code, 1792 Statute[13]

This statute detailed methods of capturing runaway servants or slaves and conveying them to prison or to their owners. Jailors' fees for committing, maintaining, and releasing runaways were noted.

The following advertisements for runaway slaves appeared in the *Virginia Gazette* (Purdie & Dixon), Williamsburg, Virginia:

- February 3, 1774, Mulatto Man Slave, slave of John Bowdoin. Northampton, captured slave.
- July 19, 1776, JOHN NEWTON, slave of William Browne. Prince William, runaway servant.
- May 19, 1776, BOB and BRISTOL,[14] slaves of John Hartwell Cocke. Swann's Point plantation in Surry County, runaway slaves.
- December 4, 1784, JOHN GRAY or JACK, slave of Charles Logan (Quaker) of Belle Meade,[15] Powhatan, VA, runaway slave.
- September 13, 1791, SAM, slave of Charles Logan of Belle Meade plantation, Powhatan, VA, runaway slave.

---

13. Thomas Costa, "Virginia Runaways: Runaway Slave Advertisements from 18th Century Virginia Newspapers," University of Virginia's College at Wise, http://jefferson.village.virginia.ed:8090/xslt/servlet/ramonvjan. XSLTServlet?xml=vcdh/XML.
"The Geography of Slavery," http://etext.lib.virginia.edu/etcbin/ot2.www-costa?specfile=/web/data/users/costa/costa.02w&.
14. More about the two slaves. On the inventory of 1771 of slaves at the Mt. Pleasant/ Swann's Point Plantation of Hartwell Cocke, inherited by John Hartwell Cocke I, Bristol and Robert are listed along with Cruso, Harry, Pompy, Hercules, Morgan, Dick, Tom, New Jack, Qually, old Jimmy, Hanniball, Rachel, Beck (b. 1765), Charlotte, Lucy, Lylna, Dinah, Rose, Issac, Annacay and daughter, Hannah, Tony, George, Sarah, Gruff, Nedd, Moses, Sucky, Fanny, and Jack.
15. Philip St. George Cocke would buy this tract of land and change it to "Belmead" in the 1830s.

3. Miscegenation, 1630 Judicial Ruling[16]

The governor and Council of Virginia ruled that Hugh Davis (white man) who was convicted of "lying with a Negro" be soundly whipped before an assembly of enslaved blacks and others for "abusing himself to the dishonor of God and shame of Christians." Punishment also included a public apology on the next Sabbath.

Miscegenation, 1640 judicial ruling

Robert Sweet, a white man, ordered to do penance in church according to the laws of England, for impregnating an enslaved black woman. The woman was ordered to be whipped by the governor and his council.

Miscegenation, 1691 statute

Any white woman in Virginia who married a black or mulatto, bond or free, was to be banished. Also Virginia outlaws interracial couples and labels their children as "that abominable mixture and spurious issue."

Miscegenation, 1847 statute

Any white person who intermarried with a black to be confined in jail up to one year and fined up to $100. and persons who performed ceremonies fined $200.

The names of *Rebecca, Becky, Beck,* or *Becca Short* and her son Robert Kennon appeared in the will of Richard Cocke Jr. (VI). They were purchased from John Hartwell Cocke II and freed immediately. He stated in his will that the whole of his estate real and personal

---

[16.] "A Very Incomplete History on Black/White Romance," http://www.cornerstonemag.com/featureb/isslll/history.htm.

(with exception of what he would give away) should be kept for the support and education of Robert Kennon.[17]

In "Surry County Virginia Register of Free Negroes" (Dennis Hudgins, Virginia Genealogical Society, 1995) chapter 22 of an act regulated to police of towns in the Commonwealth and restrained the practice of Negroes going at large (passed December 10, 1793). Chapter 23 prevented the migration of free Negroes and mulattoes into the commonwealth (passed December 12, 1793). Mulattoes and Negroes were registered and certified, making them agreeable to the acts. A description and number were issued by the county. Regarding the registry of enslaved/free blacks, an 1801 statute required tax commissioners to annually prepare a list of all free blacks and mulattoes within his district. Failure to do so resulted in a fine of $20. Free blacks who moved to another county without "honest employment" could be deemed and treated as a vagrant.

Listed among these freed Negroes by the will of Richard the Sixth were Becky Short and her two sons Richard Short and William Short. No freed Negro named Robert Kennon appeared. What happened to him—passed for white, left the state, died, met with harm, or changed his name? The following descriptions appeared for Becky (b. 1765–1773) and her two sons Richard (b. 1809) and William (b. 1811), who were born after Robert:

> *"Becky," alias "Becky Short,"* a mulatto woman *of bright complexion*, who was emancipated by William Taliaferro admor. Of Richard Cocke jun decd: by deed of emancipation bearing date the 7th day of October 1801 or 1800 and duly recorded on the 27 of the same Month. Aged 54 years last May has no scar perceiveable is 5 feet 1/2 inches high. Registered and numbered "272" this 1st day of November 1819 Pursuant to An

---

[17.] Surry County Will Book 1, p. 471.
"Virginia Slaves Freed in Virginia after 1782,"
http://www.freeafricanamericans.com/virginiafreeafter1782.htm

Act of the General Assembly of Virginia entitled An Act more effectually to restrain the practice of Negroes going at large. Register renewed this 28th May 1827. Teste W. S. Booth d.c.s.c., Teste John N. Spratley d.c.s.c.

Richard, alias Richard Short, son of Rebecca Short a free woman of this County who was emancipated by William Taliaferro Admon of Richard Cocke jr. decd. By deed of emancipation dated 7th day of October 1801. The said Richard short was born free, is of a light complexion, has a scar on the right side of his chin, the said Richard Short will be 19 years of age the 31st day of May next, and is 5 feet, 5 and 1/2 inches high. Registered of the above description and numbered 357. In the office of Surry County the 2nd day of January 1828. Teste Walter S. Booth d.c.s.c., (p. 151, #358)

William, alias William Short, son of Rebecca Short—a free woman of this County, who was emancipated by William Taliaferro Admor of Richard Cocke junr. Decd. By deed of emancipation dated 7th day of October 1801. the said William Short was born free is of a light complexion, has a scar on the right side of the face near the ear, the said William Short will be 17 years of age the 8th day of August next; and 5 feet, 1 inch high. Registered of the above description and numbered 358 in the Office of Surry County the 2nd. Day of January 1828. Teste, Walter S. Booth d.c.s.c.

Other listed in the will of Richard Cocke Jr. by deeds of emancipation were the following:

- *Ceasar Cocke* (b. 1785), a black man aged about forty-eight years
- *Moses Sturtevant Turner*, a Negro man rather of bright complexion
- *Aggy Turner* (b. 1757), a Negro woman of rather a bright complexion
- *Paul Jones* (b. 1772), a Negro man of a very dark complexion
- *Simon Turner* (b. 1796), a Negro man, rather of a bright complexion
- *Jacob Clayton Turner* (b. 1800), a free man of color

In "The historical Background of the Mount Pleasant-Swann's Point Tract, Surry County, Virginia," Martha W. McCartney states that the most remarkable features of Richard Cocke VI's will were the bequests he made to his slave Becky (Rebecca) and her son Robert Kennon, whom he acknowledged as his own child. In a departure from tradition, the testator gave to Becky, the woman bought of John Hartwell Cocke II, the sum of (#12) a year for support as long as she kept single and did not breed. He then went on to say, "Now all and every part of my property whatsoever not heretofore mentioned I give to my child Robert Kennon on his attaining the age of 21 years." He stated that if Robert Kennon failed to attain the age of twenty-one, the watch, bed, gun, tool chest, optical glass, book of prints, breast pin, and stud he stood to inherit were to be given to Walter Taliaferro. The remainder of Robert Kennon's inheritance was to be sold and divided equally among the testator's three sisters, each of whom had to pay $333.33 to Richard Cocke Archer, the testator's godson, when he attained age twenty-one. Richard Cocke VI designated Nicholas Faulcon, William Taliaferro, and John Hartwell Cocke II as his executors and asked his friend William Taliaferro to "take my child Robert Kennon under his particular direction and to have him brought up as he may judge most proper." Taliaferro was to have beef, pork, fowls, and other products from his estate as compensation for taking care of Robert. Richard Cocke VI died sometime prior to January 24, 1801, at which time his will was presented to Surry County's court justices.[18]

> Whereas Richard Cocke Jr late of Surry dec'd did by his last will and testament among other things direct that the woman Becca and her son Robert Kennon which I have bought of John H. Cocke paid 100L as per receipt shall be free immediately and whereas the said John H. Cocke who was at that time in his infancy has since attained the age of 21 and has by deed bearing date 26 Oct 01 released all right etc., so William Taliaferro admin of will of Richard Cocke frees said woman Becky and her child Robert Kennon—27 Oct 1801—rec same.

Whereas Richard Cocke Jr late of the county of Surry decd did by his last will and testament bearing date 4 Oct 1800 and duly recorded directed that the whole of my estate real and personal except what I give away should be kept together under the direction of my execs heretofore named for the support and education of Robert Kennon until the said Robt Kennon shall attain the age of 21 yrs or until his death whichever shall first happen, if the latter it is my desire that my execs do emancipate and set free all my Negroes above the age of 21 (males) or 18 (females) and others when they reach majorities; but if the said Robt Kennon should live to attain the age of 21 then I desire the Negroes may be freed in the same manner except

---

[18.] "Surry County, Virginia, Wills" (1800-1804): 471–473.

Martha W. McCartney, Mount Pleasant Restoration, "The Historical Background of the Mount Pleasant-Swann's Point Tract. Surry County, Virginia," http://www.mountpleasantrestoration.com/html/resear/mcc/hist-14.html.

Surry County Deed Book No. 2, 1799–1804, LVA Reel #19, p. 191.
Surry County Deed Book No. 5, 1815–1818, LVA Reel # 21, p. 361.
Surry County Will Book No. 1, 1792–1804, LVA Reel #8, p. 471.

said Robt Kennon shou'd keep the young ones until they arrive to the ages first for their freedom by me and no longer—and since W. Taliaferro, one of the execs has lately died and the admin of estate of Richard Cocke has been granted to Eliza Hartwell Taliaferro of Caroline County and since Robt Kennon has lately ie on 8 April turned 21, she frees the slave all above the age of 21 viz: Beck, Aggy, Paul, Caesar and Simon all of which have been in Surry since death of Richard Cocke—29 April 1817, rec 7 May 1817.

> Richard Cocke Jr. secondly that the woman Becky and her son Robert Kennon which I have bought of John Hartwell Cocke and paid one hundred pounds for as per receipt shall be free immediately, then I request that the whole of my estate real and personal except what I shall particularly give away should be kept together under the direction of my executor hereafter named for the support and education of Robert Kennon until the said attain the age of twenty one years or until his death whichever shall first happen, if the latter it is my desire that my executors do emancipate or set free all my Negroes above the age of twenty one years the males and the females above the age of eighteen years, keeping those under such ages until they arrive to the same, and as they may to be freed in the same manner as the others, but if the said Robert Kennon should live to attain the age of twenty one years, then I desire the Negroes may be freed in the same manner except that Robert Kennon should keep the young ones until they arrive to the ages fixt for their freedom by me and no longer—4 Oct 00-rec 24 Feb 01)[19]

---

19. "Virginia Slaves Freed in Virginia after 1782," http://www.freeafricanamericans.com/virginiafreeafter1782.htm

The following are Negroes emancipated by the 1799 Will of William Browne of Four Mile Tree on the death of his daughter Sally Edwards (Browne) Bowdoin in 1815:

- *Mary Ann Jones* (b. 1798), a Negro woman of a remarkable bright complexion for a Negro
- *William Hamilton Browne* (b. 1800), a Negro boy of a bright complexion
- *Sally Ann Sturtevant* (b. 1800), a small Negro woman of a bright color for a Negro
- *Robert Henry Skipwith* (b. 1801), a Negro boy of a very bright yellow complexion
- *Bevely Rowser Shipwith* (b. 1802), a Negro boy of a very bright complexion, or yellow complexion, pretty full eyes, long but not straight hair
- *Jordan Browne* (b. 1802), a Negro boy, (very black) dark complexion
- *Armistead Willis Skipwith* (b. 1804), a Negro boy of a very bright complexion, has straight hair, and much the appearance of a mulatto

William Browne of Surry

I emancipate and set free my servant Simon and old Gilly. The latter I desire may remain on the plantation during her life and be supported out of my estate—I give and bequeath to my daughter Sally during her life the following Negroes, to wit. Woodley, Silvia and her children, namely Jenny, Rose, Moses, and Sally Ann, Maria, the wife of Simon and her child Mary Ann, and at the death of my said daughter I emancipate and set free the said Woodley, Silvia, Jenny, Sally Ann, Maria and her child Mary Ann, and all the future progeny of the said females and I then give and bequeath the above mentioned boy Moses to William Ruffin son of Theoderick B Ruffin and his heirs, and the aforesaid girl Rose and such issue as she may then have to Jane B. Ruffin daughter of the said Theoderick B. Ruffin and her heirs—wants his Negro man Woodley to be kept by Nicholas Faulcon as a hostler or hired out for that purpose as the said Faulcon may think proper—other provisions for slaves to be kept together until distributed to William Browne son of Henry Browne late of Norfolk—also wants Simon to continue at plantation with Faulcon but if latter chooses not to live there then execs to get some decent and discreet person to live there and for Simon to continue to assist in taking care of the house and furniture and to be paid annually a compensation equal to his services—14 Nov 99, rec Dec 24 99. (Surry County Will Book No. 1, 1792–1804, LVA Reel 8, p. 361)[20]

4. Manumission and Experiments

- *Manumission (1691 statute).* To limit the increase of free black manumission required special legislative acts.
- *Manumission (1782 statute).* Removed restrictions on voluntary manumissions. The law was repealed five years later (1787).
- *Emancipation (1826 statute).* No black, age twenty-one or older, emancipated since May 1, 1806, to remain more than one year in the state without lawful permission.
- *Emancipation (1831 statute).* Free blacks and mulattoes remaining in the state contrary to the law, to be sold.

[20.] Ibid.

- *Re-enslavement (1851 Constitution).* Provided that emancipated blacks would be enslaved again if they did not leave the state within twelve months.
- *Voluntary enslavement (1856 statute).* Blacks given the right to enslave themselves by petition to the legislature to a master of their choosing. A master would pay the court one half the valuation of the black.
- *Emancipation (1856 statute).* Any person may emancipate any of his blacks by last will in writing or deed. All those emancipated were liable for any debt by the person emancipating them before such emancipation would take effect.
- *Emancipation (1860 Constitution).* Emancipated blacks would forfeit their freedom by remaining in the state more than twelve months. Furthermore, the General Assembly would not emancipate any enslaved person or the descendant of any such person.
- *Enslavement outlawed (1865 Constitution).* Enslavement and involuntary servitude outlawed.
- *Enslavement outlawed (1865 statute).* Certain acts relating to enslavement repealed.
- *Children of enslaved (1872 Constitution).* Children of enslaved parents entitled to inheritance as though their parents had been legally married.

The American Anti-Slavery Society (AASS), 1833–1870, was an abolitionist society founded by William Lloyd Garrison and Arthur Tappan. It called for the immediate abolition of slavery without terms and was critical of the American Colonization Society.[21]

Two abolistionists, Gerrit Smith and John Brown, were part of this movement—Gerrit Smith for his upstate New York Experiment at "North Elba" and John Brown's Harpers Ferry (VA) Raid. John Brown was a resident of North Elba. One biographer of John Brown said Brown played a part in killing slavery, sparking the Civil War

---

[21.] "American Colonization Society," *Wikipedia*, https://en.wikipedia.org/wiki/American Colonization Society.

and seeding civil rights. Another called Brown "an American who gave his life so that millions of other Americans might be free."

Gerrit Smith and the North Elba Experiment (New York)

Gerrit Smith (1797–1874), abolitionist, was born near Syracuse, New York. He was wealthy. He inherited immense real estate holdings of more than one million acres in Virginia, Pennsylvania, and New York.

His father, Peter Smith, Sr., founded the town of Peterboro in 1795, naming it after himself. He was an early partner of John Jacob Astor in the fur business. His father invested in acreage throughout the Alleghanies, Mohawk Valley, and Adirondacks.

Gerrit Smith was religious and helped support Polish and Greek refugees, Irish famine victims, industrial training schools for the blind, Oswego Free Library, and the antislavery newspaper, the *North Star*, of Frederick Douglass (African American abolitionist).

Smith's ideology shifted. He was one of the founders of the antislavery Liberty Party in 1840. He was elected to Congress in 1852 but later resigned. He endorsed African repatriation and compensated emancipation like his friend John Hartwell Cocke II of Virginia. Later he rejected both. He believed in the Liberty Party's idea of working nonviolently through political action within the system and under the Constitution to bring slavery to an end. He affiliated himself with the revolutionary John Brown.

In 1838, Smith donated twenty-one thousand undeveloped acres in Western Virginia (now West Virginia) to the abolitionist Oberlin College. (My husband's grandmother Bessie [Gibson] Kemp graduated from this college with a degree in music.) John Brown was contracted to survey Smith's land grant (1840)—eight years prior to meeting Smith. Brown came to know the rugged trans-Ohio backcountry where he would foment revolution.

Smith, as an opponent of land monopoly, gave numerous farms of 50 acres each to indigent families, totaling 200,000 acres. In 1846,

Smith set aside 120,000 acres of land in New York's Adirondack Mountains to be parceled into homesteads for black freedmen at North Elba, near Lake Placid in Essex County, New York. Of a forecasted 3,000 families, 1,985 were given 40-acre plots. The goal was to give the blacks a new beginning but also to qualify them to vote under New York State's property qualification of net assets representing at least $250 in value. The blacks had a hard time at North Elba (also called *Timbucto*). The north land and the climate were different from the growing methods in the south. Negroes lacked construction skills (houses and barns). They faced harassment, sabotage, and discrimination from the whites. The Negroes ended up destitute, hungry, and shelterless. The project failed.

Before meeting Smith in 1848, John Brown offered in an introductory letter to take one of the farms himself; clear and plant it and show his colored neighbors how much work should be done; give them work; look after them; and be a kind father to them because he had grown up among the woods and Indians of Ohio and was used to the climate and the way of life that the colony at North Elba found so trying.

Besides donating land and money to the African American community in North Elba, New York, Smith was involved in the temperance movement—he built one of the first temperance hotels in the country—and later the colonization movement. As a staunch abolitionist, Smith was a member of the Secret Six, who financially supported John Brown's raid at Harpers Ferry, West Virginia. He was first cousin to Elizabeth Cady Stanton, a founder of and leader of the Women's Suffrage Movement, which he supported.

Later Peterboro became a station on the Underground Railroad. After 1850, Smith furnished money for the legal defense of persons charged with violating the Fugitive Slave Law and the Kansas Aid Movement (a campaign to raise money and solidarity with antislavery immigrants to that territory). During this movement, he first met and financially supported John Brown. Later he sold a farm in North Elba to Brown and supported him with funds. In 1859, Smith joined the Secret Six, a group of influential northern abolitionist, who supported John Brown in his efforts to capture the Armory at Harpers Ferry, West Virginia (then Virginia) and arm the slaves.[22]

John Brown and the Harpers Ferry, Virginia Raid

John Brown was born on May 9, 1780 in Torrington, Connecticut, and was the grandson of Captain John Brown. Brown could trace his ancestry back to the seventeenth-century English Puritans. He was married two times and had twenty children (eleven survived to adulthood). Ulysses S. Grant's father was an apprentice to Brown's father. John Brown operated a successful tannery business in Hudson, Ohio. About 1820, Brown and his family moved to Pennsylvania where he operated a tannery, raised cattle, and worked as a surveyor. Later (1836) he moved to Franklin Mills (Kent), Ohio, and operated a tannery along with horses and sheep breeding.

In 1846, Brown moved to Springfield, Massachusetts, and set up a wool commission operation. While in Springfield, Brown transformed the city into a major city of abolitionism and one of the safest and most significant stops on the Underground Railroad. Brown founded the League of Gileadites, a militant group formed to prevent slaves capture in response to the US Fugitive Slave Act, which required authorities in free states to aid in the return of escaped slaves and imposed penalties on those who aided in their escape. He also found sources for the future financial support that he would receive from New England's great merchants and met nationally famous abolitionists like Frederick Douglass and Sojourner Truth. In 1848, Brown heard of Gerrit Smith's Adirondack land grant to poor black men and decided to move his family among them. He bought 244 acres of land near North Elba, New York, for $1 an acre and spent two years there.

In 1855, Brown learned that his family members in Kansas Territory were unprepared to face attacks and that the proslavery forces there were militant. To protect his family and oppose the

22. "Gerrit Smith," *Wikipedia*, https://en/wikipedia.org/wiki/Gerrit Smith.

advances of slavery supporters, Brown left for Kansas with funds and guns. Brown and the free settlers were optimistic that they could bring Kansas into the Union as a slave-free state. (During this time, Preston Brooks caned antislavery senator Charles Sumner in the US Senate.)

In 1856, the massacre at Pottawatomie occurred. When a force of Missourians attacked a settlement at Palmyra, Kansas, Brown and his men successfully defended the settlement. Later a company of Missourians attempted to destroy the settlement (free state) of Osawatomie. Brown and his men attempted to defend the settlement but were outnumbered and had to flee. The Missourians plundered and burned the settlement. Brown's bravery and military shrewdness in the face of overwhelming odds brought him national attention and made him a hero to many Northern abolitionists. Shortly thereafter, Brown left Kansas to raise money from supporters in the North. Brown's son Frederick was killed.

In 1857 a group of six wealthy abolitionists—Franklin Sanborn, Thomas Wentworth Higginson (helped muster black troops during the Civil War), Theodore Parker, George Luther Stearns, Samuel Gridley Howe, and Gerrit Smith—agreed to offer Brown financial support for his antislavery activities. They would eventually provide most of the financial backing for the raid on Harpers Ferry, and they would become known as the Secret Six and the Committee of Six.[23]

Many abolitionists believed that blacks were inferior to whites in intellectual power. They opposed slavery as a concept. A few blacks were considered exception to the rule of black inferiority. Julia Ward Howe, wife of one of the Secret Six, Dr. Samuel Gridley Howe, who became the first in the world to teach language to a blind-deaf mute, described how the "ideal Negro" would be one "refined by white culture, elevated by white blood." She wrote:

> [N]egro upon negroes is a course, grinning, flat-footed, thick skulled creature, ugly as Caliban,

---

[23.] Edward J. Renehan Jr., *The Secret Six: The True Tale of the Men Who Conspired with John Brown* (South Carolina: University of South Carolina Press, 1995).

lazy as the laziest brutes, chiefly ambitious to be
of no use to any in the world… He must go to
school to the white race and his discipline must
be long and laborious.

During Reconstruction and after, many Northern whites moved
South to take advantage of the newly freed slave population and the
destitute planters. They were known as carpetbaggers.

Thomas W. Higginson, militant New England abolitionist,
commanded the first freed slaves to fight against the Confederacy.
He recorded the songs sung by the First South Carolina Volunteers
sitting around evening campfires. They include the following: "Hold
Your Light," "Bound to Go," "Room in There," "Hail Mary," "My
Army Cross Over," "Ride In, Kind Saviour," "This World Almost
Done," "I Want to Go Home," "The Coming Day," "One More
River," "The Dying Lamb!," "Down in the Valley," "Cry Holy,"
"O'er the Crossing," "Walk 'em Easy," "O Yes, Lord," "Blow Low,
Mary," "I Know Moon Rise," "Wrestling Jacob," "The Baby Gone
Home," "Lord, Remember Me," "Early in the Morning," "Go in the
Wilderness," "Blow Your Trumpet Gabriel," "In the Morning," "Fare
Ye Well," "The Ship of Zion," "The Ship of Zion" (second version
and third version), "Sweet Music," "Good News," "We'll Soon Be
Free," "Many Thousand Go," "The Driver," and "Hangman Johnny"
(thirty-nine songs).[24]

The 1858 elections saw a free-state victory for Kansas. Brown
went to Springdale, Iowa, to plan his Virginia scheme. Next he went
to Canada (Chatham, Ontario). Here he met Harriet Tubman.
One-third of the population were fugitive slaves. Brown returned to
Kansas and Missouri.

On March 1859, Brown met with Frederick Douglass and
other abolitionists to discuss emancipation. During the next few

---

[24.] Milton C. Servett, ed., "Chapter 2: Slave Religion in the Antebellum South, section 13: 'Thomas Wentworth Higginson: Slave Songs and Spirituals,'" in *African American Religious History: A Documentary Witness* (Durham: Duke University Press, 1985).

months, he traveled through Ohio, New York, Connecticut, and Massachusetts to draw up more support for the cause and reconnoitered with the Secret Six. In June 1859, he paid his last visit to his family in North Elba before he departed for Harpers Ferry.

Harriet Tubman (referred to as "General Tubman" by Brown) joined Brown in planning an attack of slaveholders. She was knowledgeable of support networks and resources in the border states of Pennsylvania, Maryland, and Delaware, which were invaluable to Brown. She gathered former slaves living in present-day Southern Ontario who were willing to join his fighting forces.

Brown arrived in Harpers Ferry, July 3, 1859. In August, he met with Douglass to reveal his plan and to plea for his support. Douglass rejected the plea and earlier had discouraged blacks from enlisting. A few days later, he rented a house in nearly Maryland. He awaited the arrival of his recruits and supplies. On October 16, 1859, Brown led his attack on the Harpers Ferry Armory. Initially, the raid went well, and they met no resistance entering the town. Things started to go wrong when an eastbound train approached the town. A battle ensued with casualties. The train continued on it way and sent a telegram telling of the raid, which reached Baltimore and the District of Columbia. The raiders were pinned down in the armory. A daylong battle ensued between the raiders and the militia. Brown sent his sons Watson and Oliver with another supporter out under a white flag. They were shot. His two sons died.

On October 18, 1859, the building was surrounded by a company of US Marines under the overall command of Colonel Robert E. Lee of the US Army. Lieutenant J. E. B. Stuart approached under a white flag, offering to spare the raiders' lives if they would surrender. Brown and the survivors were captured when Brown refused to surrender. Five of his men escaped, including his son Owen. Brown and others captured were held in the office of the armory. A three-hour questioning session took place. They were tried on October 27, 1859, in Virginia in Charles Town, nearby county seat of Jefferson County. Brown was charged with murdering four whites and a black, with conspiring with slaves to rebel, and with treason against Virginia.

On October 31, 1859, Hiram Griswold, Brown's attorney, in his closing statement, argued that Brown could not be found guilty of treason against the state to which he owed no loyalty and of which he was not a resident, and that Brown had not personally killed anyone himself and also that the failure of the raid indicated that Brown had not conspired with the slaves.

On November 2, 1859, after a weeklong trial and forty-five minutes of deliberation, the Charles Town jury found Brown guilty on all three counts. Brown was sentenced to be hanged in public on December 2. Cadets from the Virginia Military Institute under the leadership of General Francis H. Smith and Major Thomas J. Jackson (two years later he would earn the nickname *Stonewall*) were called into service as a security detail in the event Brown's supporters attempted a rescue. Philip St. George Cocke (1809–1861) organized a Powhatan cavalry troop that drilled in 1860 in response to John Brown's raid in Harpers Ferry.[25]

During his month in jail, Brown was allowed to receive and send correspondence. Brown refused to be rescued by a Kansas friend who had gotten into the Jefferson County jail and offered to break him out during the night and flee northward. Brown preferred to die as a martyr. On December 1, Brown's wife came to Harpers Ferry and joined him for the last meal at the jail. Victor Hugo tried to obtain pardon for John Brown. Brown wrote the following on the morning of December 2, 1859:

> I John Brown, am now quite certain that the crimes of this guilty land will never be purged away but with blood. I had, as I now think, vainly flatter myself that without very much bloodshed it might be done.

He read his Bible, wrote a final letter to his wife, and wrote his will. At 11:00 a.m., he was escorted from the jail to a small field

---

[25] "Cocke, Philip St. George (1809–1861)," http://www.encyclopediavirginia. org/Cocke Philip St. George 1909–1861.

where the gallows were placed for execution. Among the crowd of two thousand soldiers were future Confederate general Stonewall Jackson and John Wilkes Booth (disguised in a militia uniform). Brown was accompanied by the sheriff and his assistants to the scaffold. He was hanged at 11:15 a.m. and pronounced dead at 11:50 a.m. Two of his sons were also hanged. His coffin was put on a train to take it to his family homestead in New York for burial. In the North, Brown was praised—memorial meetings, ringing church bells, firing of minute guns, and writers supporting slave insurrection.

On December 14, 1859, the US Senate appointed a bipartisan committee to investigate the Harpers Ferry raid and to determine whether any citizens contributed arms, ammunition, or money to John Brown's men. The report was published in June 1860. It found no direct evidence of a conspiracy but implied that the raid was a result of Republican doctrines. The South recognizing their decrepit militia system reorganized and established a ready-made Confederate Army by 1861. Harpers Ferry raid in 1859 escalated tension that a year later led to secession and the American Civil War. Brown's actions made him a controversial figure—he is memorialized as a heroic martyr and sometimes vilified as a madman and a terrorist.[26]

The Society for the Colonization of Free People of Color of America, commonly known as the American Colonization Society (ACS), was a group established in 1816 by Robert Finley of New Jersey which supported the migration of free African Americans to the continent of Africa. It helped found the colony of Liberia in 1821–22 on the coast of West Africa as a place for free-born American blacks.[27]

Two Cocke family members, John Hartwell Cocke II (Mount Pleasant Plantation, Surry County, Virginia; Bremo Plantations, Fluvanna County, Virginia; and Mount Hope Plantation, Alabama) and his sister Sally Cocke Faulcon (Mount Pleasant Plantation, Surry County, Virginia), were associated with this movement. John

---

[26]. "John Brown," *Wikipedia*, https://en/wikipedia.org/wiki/John Brown (abolitionist).
[27]. "American Colonization Society," *Wikipedia*, https://en.wikipedia.org/wiki/ American Colonization Society.

Hartwell sent a group of freed African Americans to Liberia. Later he implemented an experiment at Mount Hope plantation in Alabama to prepare enslaved blacks to gain their freedom for emigration to Liberia. Sally Faulcon offered freedom to her "outright ownership" slaves if they chose to go to Liberia in her will of 1831. Two enslaved blacks were manumitted by Philip St. George Cocke (proslaver) so that they could join their family in Liberia.

John Hartwell Cocke and the Hopewell Experiment (Alabama)

By 1835, Cocke was proposing the use of Southern cotton lands to earn the funds for Negro liberation. The same year, Thomas Napier offered Cocke the use of a thousand acres in Florida for his experiment. Cocke declined the offer. He instead suggested, two years later, to his son Charles to execute a plan. Cocke stated that the enterprise would involve taking fifty, seventy-five, or one hundred Negroes to the cotton country of the Southwest or Florida, after realizing their value there, use the surplus to give them an outfit in Africa, and pay their passage thither to return them to the land of their forefathers. Charles showed no interest in the venture. Cocke confided this scheme to his friend and onetime protégé of Jefferson, William Short of Philadelphia. Short was a moderate opponent of slavery. His letters often spoke of ideas regarding emancipation. He told Cocke in one letter (1837) that Cocke's plan of liberation seems to be "the best I have heard of" and wished him success.

In 1839, Gerrit Smith (abolitionist and millionaire of Peterboro, New York) urged his friend John Hartwell Cocke to free his Virginia slaves. Cocke believed that blacks should be liberated and leave the country and supported the ACS mission. In 1840, Gerrit Smith, former supporter of colonization, asked Cocke to emancipate his slaves. Smith proposed giving twenty-five acres in New York to each slave Cocke emancipated. Cocke rejected the offer and told Smith that he had a better plan. Cocke had formulated and had underway an

Experiment in Emancipation. Cocke continued his ties with his old friend. He dined with Gerrit Smith in Washington, DC, in May 1854 and recorded that the millionaire of Peterboro was "certainly a man of the most interesting character and fine abilities." (Five years later, Smith financed John Brown's activities at Harpers Ferry.) Cocke had a great respect for the "North," excluding the abolitionists. John Hartwell made the following comments:

> Our improvements come from the North (1838); thank God the Yankees are at hand (1844); Northerners are the greatest people on Earth (1854); Yankee brotheren are beyond comparison…the best part of our Nation (1860); as to the ultraclique of abolitionists, they are as much dispised here, among the good and true men as they are with us (1860).

Cocke referred to Frederick Douglass as the "notorious darky" when Northern abolitionists attempted to introduce their agenda into the anti-liquor proceedings during the World Temperance Convention in New York in 1853. Cocke's love for the North was contingent upon his conviction of its moderation toward slaveholders.

Philip St. George Cocke's response to the institution of slavery was expressed in terms of, "Long! Long! May the South Retain Slavery (1852). I for one complain not of slavery, but Thank God that I and my children have been placed in the midst of it." His father commented on how he had witnessed Philip's family on a visit to the Virginia Springs in 1853 squander money. John Hartwell termed it as "more money was spent than would support a missionary in China!"[28]

[28.] John Hartwell Cocke II, Journal (1853–54), May 26,1854, Shields Deposit.
Letter from Gerrit Smith to John H. Cock, December 11,1840, Cocke Deposit.
Letter draft from John Hartwell Cocke II to Gerrit Smith, December 13,1839, Shields Deposit.
Undated, untitled letter draft to Gerrit Smith, Cocke Deposit.

Prior to Cocke's "Experiment in Emancipation," which he referred to in response to Gerrit Smith's offer of acreage to each of the slaves Cocke freed, Cocke had liberated in 1833 a number of slaves to Liberia under the leadership of Peyton Skipwith (son of Lucy and Jessie Skipwith). The Liberian settlers included Samuel Benedict, Stephen Allen Benson, James Byrd, Peter and Richard Cannon, George Cocke, Reed Cooper, Solomon Creasy, Agnes Faulcon, Ann Sucky Faulcon, John Faulcon, Sion Harris, Green Haskin, Moore James, William Andrew Johnson, David Logan, Eliza Adala Lomax, Lydia Ann Lomax, Samuel Lomax, James B. McGill, Erasmus Nicholas, James Nicholas, Julia Nicholas, James Sims, Diana Skipwith, Felicia Skipwith, James Skipwith, Lydia Skipwith, Margaret (Skinner) Skipwith, Martha Skipwith (Peyton's daughter), Matilda Skipwith, Napolean Skipwith, Nash Skipwith, Peyton Skipwith, Feny Smith, Harrison Story, Diana Sturdivant, Leander Sturdivant, Leander (younger) Sturdivant, and Rosetta Sturdivant.

A number of Cocke's slaves in Fluvanna County, Virginia (Bremo Plantation), were readied to participate in the Alabama Experiment. They were expected to learn agricultural and industrial skills, letters, 3 Rs, and practice religious principles—no alcohol/drinking, smoking, dishonesty, etc. They were expected to work five to seven years to buy their freedom (estimated at about $1,400 to $3,000).

In the past, holidays were observed: Easter Monday, Whitsunday, Thanksgiving, wheat harvest completion week of rest, and Christmas (three to seven days) with dinners and gifts from the master. Cocke disqualified one group from participation in the experiment: the James River watermen/river boatmen. He said that they were the worst class of Negroes who the master rid themselves of the "idle, refractory, and thievish by hiring them out to this occupation where they must readily get a fair hire for their labour." He prohibited the servants from receiving and entertaining with them because of their bad character and reputation as purchasers of stolen goods. The river

Coyner Jr., Martin Boyd, "John Hartwell Cocke of Bremo: Agriculture and Slavery in the Antebellum South," doctoral dissertation (University of Virginia, 1961).

between Richmond and Lynchburg (130 miles) served two or three thousands boatmen. Cocke said the majority were slaves, and the white watermen were also for the most part of the lowest and most disreputable class.

According to Cousin Julian F. Burke IV, African American genealogist, one boatman in our African American Carrington lineage was Washington Saunders/Sanderson (born June 1832 on Tuckahoe Plantation and later settled in Cartersville, Cumberland County, Virginia). As an adult, he ferried bateau boats up and down the James River carrying supplies. The profession was a prominent one, even among the white Sanderson men. This profession was very important to the economy before the completion of the James River and Kanawha Canal.

In 1840, George Skipwith, slave driver/foreman and son of Jessie and Lucy (Nichols) Skipwith, took a group (forty-nine slaves) to Hopewell Plantation in Green County, Alabama. They left Bremo and walked seven weeks. The experiment was managed by Cocke's agent Abraham Perkins and Elam Tanner, perspective overseer.

Bremo Plantation's enslaved African Americans included the following: Chapman, Charles, Shadrach Cocke, Archer Creasy (Foreman), Benjamin Creasy, Betty Creasy, James Creasy, Lavinia (Skipwith) Creasy, Leander Creasy, Jessie Dabney, Daniel, Dinah, Berthier Edwards, Felicia Edwards, Ned Edwards, Daphne (Faulcon) Drew, Isham Gault, Julyann Gault, Godfrey, Harriet, Armistead Hewitt (Foreman), Janis, Lucy Johnson, Marcia Johnson, Qually Johnson, Lisa Kellor, Sam Kellor, Spencer Kellor, Violley, Washington and Ned Washington, William, Henry (mason), Charlotte (Morse) Lewis, Robert Lewis, Mike, Morris, Nancy, Lucy Nicholas, Albert Morse,[29] Ann Morse, Betsey Morse, Cain Morse, Carter Morse, Champion Morse, Charles Morse, Jinney Morse, Kessiah Morse, Martha (Skipwith) Morse (George's daughter), Matilda Morse, Matthew Morse, Rebecca (Bird) Morse, Sandy Morse, Betsey Randall, Frank Randall, Jinny Randall, Primus Randall, Sally, Scipio, Berthier Skipwith, Betsey Skipwith, Dinah Skipwith, George Skipwith, Little

---

[29.] The surname *Morse* is also spelled as *Morris* or *Moss*.

George Skipwith, Gerry Skipwith, Howell Skipwith, Isaetta Skipwith, Jessie Skipwith, Lucy Skipwith, Maria Skipwith, Mary Skipwith, old Mary Skipwith, Patsy Skipwith, Polly (Brown) Skipwith, Richard Skipwith, William Skipwith, and Evelina Smith.

Only fourteen from Alabama went to Liberia. In 1850, Cocke sent out another group of twenty-three candidates for emigration to Liberia, West Africa.[30]

Sally (Cocke) Faulcon and the 1831 will (Enslavement in America or Freedom as Emigrants to Liberia, West Africa)

John Hartwell Cocke II's sister, Sally (Cocke) Faulcon, also supported the American Colonization Society movement like her brother. In her will, she offered her slaves enslavement in America or freedom as emigrants to Liberia, West Africa. Her husband, Nicholas Faulcon of Mount Pleasant, Surry County, Virginia, died in 1826 and left her "life rights" in twenty-five slaves: old Hailey, James Hailey, his wife Betsy, and daughter Betsy; Ned; Davy; Dianna and her four children (Evelyn, Cornelius, Scipio, and Becky); Lucy and her daughter Angelina; Levinia and her two children (Eliza and Anthony); Alfred; Nelly; Little Moses; Polly Low; Jenny Low; Daniel; Werther; Abram; Peter Culpepper; Tillah Griffin; William Griffin; Almira; old Sarah; and old Nancy. He also left life rights in all of those females' slave children. He specified that upon Sally's death, all the life-rights slaves were to be sold, and the proceeds of the slave sale were to go to his relatives, except the slaves old Hailey and Lucy and her daughter. Nicholas Faulcon left "outright ownership" of twenty-eight slaves to his wife: old Dinah, Molly and her son Leander, Inez and all her

---

[30.] Randall M. Miller, ed., "Dear Master: Letters of a Slave Family" (University of Georgia Press, 1990).

Coyner Jr., Martin Boyd, "John Hartwell Cocke of Bremo: Agriculture and Slavery in the Antebellum South," doctoral dissertation (University of Virginia, 1961).

Julian F. Burke IV, *Lest We Forget: A Tribute to My Ancestors* (1998).

children and grandchildren (Lisa Jones and her three children), Sally, Simon, Mary, Ned, Billy, Peter Jones, Mary, Patsy, Richard, Jenny, Sucky, Lucy and Judy, Melvinia and her two children (James Henry and John), and Henry (Melvinia's husband).

Sally had made a will in 1831. In the will, she left her faithful servant Molly Sturdivant household furniture, furnishings, and food. She left the other house servants home furnishings and clothing. She liberated Molly Sturdivant if she would leave the state or she could remain a slave in the state of Virginia and live with Sally's relatives of Molly's choosing who would provide her with a comfortable house. She also gave Molly $400 to be paid in five years, whether she stayed in Virginia or left. She also liberated Molly's son Leander, his wife, and children. She gave them the option of remaining in Virginia as slaves and choosing masters among her relatives. She wanted all of her slaves to go to Liberia, if willing. If they wished to remain in Virginia, they should choose masters among her relatives. She requested that Molly's granddaughter Mary Diane remain with Molly for the rest of Molly's life. If Diana's parents chose to go to Liberia, then Diana would go with them. She also requested that her servants going to Liberia be made comfortable for the journey. She made provisions for taking care of her sick and elderly (nonworking) servants through money set aside for charitable purposes by her relatives who would become their masters.[31]

Sally Cocke Faulcon died on November 14, 1840, in an accident near Belmead when the carriage was overturned, and she was seriously injured. She died before she could be reached. She was on her way to Goochland to attend a church service.

The enslaved African Americans of Sally who elected freedom and emigration to Liberia, West Africa, to slavery in American were the following: James Nicholas, Judy Nicholas, Richard Cannon, Peter Jones (paralyzed), Leander Sturdivant, Diane Sturdivant, Rose Sturdivant, Susan, and Mary. James Nicholas, Dick Cannon,

---

[31.] Cocke Manuscripts 640, Box 99, University of Virginia, Small Collection.
Surry County Will Book 8 (1840–1845): 109-111; 435-436.
Surry County Order Book (1838–1843):187–188.

Peter Jones, and Judy Nicholas each received $50. On June 1, 1842, they boarded the steamer Thomas Jefferson in Richmond. Then in Norfolk, they boarded the *Mariposa*, which took them to Liberia. Philip St. George Cocke manumitted Erasmus Nicholas and Sally Taylor so that they could be with their families in Liberia.[32]

5. Education Codes

- *Education (1805 statute)*. Blacks or mulatto orphans not to be taught, reading, writing or arithmetic.
- *Education (1831 statute)*. Act prohibited meetings to teach free blacks to read or write. The penalty on white persons who offered such instruction was $50. White persons who taught enslaved blacks were to be fined between $10 and $100.
- *Education (1832 statute)*. Illegal to teach enslaved blacks how to read and write. Fine of $10 to $100. Law was strictly enforced unlike earlier literacy laws.

At Bremo, Cocke's second wife instructed the slaves in reading and in religious matters during the 1820s. Cocke later hired teachers from the North to conduct a more formal school for the slaves, although his wife resumed her duties when Virginia outlawed the employment of teachers for blacks in 1831. He had married Louisa Maxwell Holmes of Norfolk (widow) five years after the death of his first wife in 1816. Louisa was a Presbyterian who aided Bible, missionary, and colonization organizations. She shared in Cocke's spiritual and philanthropic pursuits and commitment to spreading the influence of Christianity. Cocke was a member of New York–

---

[32]. "Emigrants by the Ship Mariposa," Capt. Shute sailed from Norfolk, June 1, 1842.
American Colonization Society, Records, Series VI. Vol. 15, Reel 314 (no page).
Mount Pleasant Plantation, "Nicholas and Sally Faulcon," http://mountpleasantplantation.com/?page id=114.

based American Tract Society, the Boston-based American Board of Commissioners for Foreign Missions, and the American Bible Society, headquartered in New York.

Cocke believed that fundamental to any scheme of moral uplift among the slaves was a system of infant schools. These Virginia and Alabama day schools used the best-trained Negro women to impart the rudiments of learning, as well as Sabbath schools for Bible instruction. At Bremo, the Sabbath school was conducted by a variety of white women, including Cocke's wife, his daughter, his daughter-in-law, and for a time, the wife of a resident chaplain. State law prohibited the employment of white teachers. He used Negro teachers for adult education and teaching reading, as well as a Wednesday-night program for instructing the boys in counting and tables of weights and measures.

The records of the American Colonization Society verify the literacy of the Bremo slaves who emigrated to Liberia. On the census of the colony of Liberia, September 1843, population of the town of Monrovia, under the category of "extent of education," Moore James, Diana James, Martha Skipwith, Julia Nichols, Matilda Skipwith, Peyton Skipwith, Harrison Story, John Faulkner are noted as able to read and write.[33]

---

[33] "Cocke John Hartwell (1780–1866)," http://www.encyclopediavirginia.org/ Cocke John Hartwell 1780–1866.

Roll of Emigrants that have been sent to the colony of Liberia, Western Africa, by the American Colonization Society and its auxiliaries, to September 1843, http://ccharitv.com/liberia/monroviacensus2.htm.

Coyner Jr., Martin Boyd, "John Hartwell Cocke of Bremo: Agriculture and Slavery in the Antebellum South," doctoral dissertation (University of Virginia, 1961).

CHAPTER 4

Finding James Morris

My great-grandfather James Morris was first a carpenter then a miller on Belmead Plantation.

On the inventory of Negroes upon Belmead Plantation taken January 1, 1854, James was listed as number 41, thirty-one years old, a carpenter, and valued at $700 (the highest value on the inventory for skilled male laborers). Carpentry was a skilled trade involving the cutting, shaping, and installation of building material during the construction of buildings, ships, timber bridges, and concrete form-works. Carpenters worked with natural wood and did the rougher work of framing. Cabinet making and furniture building were considered carpentry. Up to the end of the 1800s, carpenters framed post-and-beam buildings. James's son George (carpenter and mechanic) and grandson Ivory (carpenter and carpentry instructor) built the ferries/flats, constructed and repaired buildings, and made cabinets and furniture at St. Emma's Agricultural and Industrial Institute and in the Mohemenco community.

Later James became a miller on the Belmead Plantation. On the inventory of Negroes dated January, 1, 1861, James was listed as number 62, forty years old, and a miller. A miller operated a mill, a machine to grind crops, such as corn, wheat, or cotton into meal, flour, or ginned fiber. Milling was among the oldest of human occupations. Millers were important to the development of agriculture. James continued with his millwork after slavery and reconstruction.

One of James's daughters married a miller from Fluvanna County, Virginia. Under "Account with Mill" dated January 13 to January 18, 1889, the following appeared: "Jim Morris, 2/3 to me and balance to Jim."

The following information documents James Morris's presence on Belmead Plantation and Mohemenco hamlet during slavery/reconstruction and postreconstruction days:[34]

1. James Morris appeared in Philip St. George Cocke's Plantation and Farm Instruction Record of 1854 under the slave inventory as a carpenter. (Later, in the 1861 plantation inventory, James was listed as a miller.)

2. This record book also included rules for the operation of the plantation, daily weather conditions, and work-completion summaries. Children associated with James and Priscilla during slavery included Kitty, Tucker, Mahala, Nelly, Irena, Hailey, and an infant (nameless). Priscilla, Tucker, and Nelly appeared on the 1853–1865 death record for Belmead. Kitty and Hailey survived to adulthood. Later he fathered children with second wife, Jane Chambers. She was from Bear Garden Plantation (Buckingham County, Virginia) owned by John Hartwell Cocke II. The children included the following: Priscilla (spinster of Powhatan); Harriet (Stone of Hurt, Virginia); Parthenia (Wooling of Pittsburgh, Pennsylvania, spouse was a miller from Fluvanna County, Virginia), Molly (Pinkney of Richmond, Virginia, spouse was a minister); Virginia (Sturdivant of Richmond, Virginia, spouse was a tobacconist); George (married Annie Jane Bell of Powhatan, Virginia); and William (mar-

---

[34.] "Cocke, Philip St. George," Plantation and Farm Instruction Records, Virginia Historical Society, 1854.

Cocke Papers, Alderman Library, University of Virginia, Charlottesville, Virginia.

Federal Censuses, 1870 and 1880, Special Census, "Agriculture."

ried Mabel "Cocke" Pryor of Powhatan, Virginia). Records indicate that James had fourteen children.

3. In a letter from Napoleon B. Drew to Ms. Bettie Cocke, granddaughter of Philip St. George Cocke, Charlottesville, Virginia, James Morris is mentioned in the correspondence as asking the writer to give his regards to Ms. Cocke. (Accession H of Collection 2433-AD, AE, Box 22, 1893–1956; heading: "Napoleon B. Drew and Family")

4. A report/memo shows James Morris's crop production during Reconstruction as a sharecropper at Belmead.

5. In a ledger "Sales with Belmead," 1886, on February 20, James is credited with 35 bushels of corn for $14, and on May 7, a credit of $1.00 is given for hay.

6. Under "Acct: with Mill," on January 13 to January 18, 1889, the following appears: Jim Morris 2/3 of grist for me and bal to Jim for [?] 5 bus of corn $3.00."

7. In "Sales from Belmead," January 29, 1890: "For 1 bu wheat to James Morris $1.00."

8. In "1892 Household Expenses": "Jim Morris 6 chickens."

9. The Federal 1870 census and the Federal 1880 special (agriculture) census reveal information about James and his family and his farming activities.

Biography of James Morris

The Trades Tradition: From Miller to Milliner

James Morris was born in Surry County, Virginia, around 1820 on one of the Cocke's plantations. His mother was Rebecca. He came to Belmead (Powhatan) and Bremo (Fluvanna) plantations with Phillip St. George Cocke in the 1830s. Around 1840s/1850s, as skilled laborers, James (carpenter) and his brother, Alfred (stonemason) were involved in the construction on Belmead property. Two other brothers, Philomon and Freeman, left Surry, Virginia, but their histories are lost. Around 1860, James began a new career as a miller and found a partner, Jane Chambers, from Bear Garden Plantation in Buckingham County, Virginia. Alfred married Gabriella Bolling. Of the children born to James and Jane, several survived to adult-hood. Several of James's family members are buried in the slave por-tion of the Belmead Historical Cemetery, including Priscilla, Tucker, and Nelly.

As a Freedman/sharecropper during Reconstruction, James began labor under John Bowdoin Cocke, Phillip's son. In 1870, James's brother, Reverend Alfred Morris, founded Mount Zion Baptist Church and served as circuit minister for three other African American churches. After Reconstruction, James and Alfred pur-chased land about one-half mile from Belmead in the Mohemenco community. James's fifty-four-acre tract of land remains in the family today. James built his home, farmed his land, and continued to work as a miller on Belmead during the early days of St. Emma's Industrial and Agricultural Institute (1895 to 1970).

During the 1880s/1890s, James's brother Alfred, sister Melvina Taylor, son Hailey, daughter Priscilla, daughter-in-law, and infant granddaughter died and were buried in community church ceme-teries. Also during this period, local ministers E. T. Jefferson and Theophilus P. Harris performed marriage ceremonies for James's two sons, William and George. On Wednesday, June 25, 1902 (while James was on the "cooling board"), George married Annie Jane Bell at the residence of the parents of Annie. George was a mechanic. George's brother, William, married Mabel Cocke-Pryor on Wednesday, May 15, 1907, at Mount Zion Church. William was a farmer.

James labored on Belmead property for sixty-six years as a carpenter and miller. He died in the African American hamlet of Mohemenco, Powhatan, Virginia (Macon District) in 1902 and was buried in his homestead cemetery. The cemetery is located south of Carterville Road and west of Bell Road. James left a "legacy of Belmead ties." Two grandsons (Ivory and John) and two nephews (Winfred Taylor and Willie Sturdivant) worked as Belmead trades instructors and educated thousands of youths from across the United States for four decades. One graduate of Saint Emma's commented in 2008: "Mr. Morris, carpentry instructor, served as a role model for me and a positive influence in my life. It was the first time I observed African American men in professional roles."

Another grandson, Luther, delivered the mail using a rowboat to cross the James River at Rock Castle and was employed at Belmead for fifty years. One grandson, Ivory, and his father, George, built the ferries and passenger boats. The Saint Francis students referred to the ferry as the "Old Robert E. Lee" or the flat. According to Ivory Morris (1906–1999), two ferries were submerged in the river and tied to the bank and they are visible when the river is low. The same grandson, at age fourteen, along with his father, uncles, and other Mohemenco tradesmen, constructed the Deep Creek Dam in 1921. Ivory built the Saint Emma's power plant building and maintained the Cartersville Parish Church. Other descendants worked as tradesmen, agricultural laborers, maintenance men, and domestics, including Abel Taylor, Herbert, James (fifty years), and Webster (fifty years) at Saint Francis; Robinson Taylor, Earl, Carl, and Elton at Saint Emma's; and Waverly Taylor at Saint Francis and Saint Emma's. After the closing of Saint Emma's, Ivory and Winfred partnered in a renovation and cabinetmaking business. Many Mohemenco kitchens have cabinets constructed by the two.

Several of James Morris's granddaughters/nieces attended the Saint Emma's Parochial School (1895–1938), which was located in the old Cocke's slave chapel. Ms. Virginia Sturdivant, James's niece, was one of the teachers. Other grandchildren attended Mohemenco Colored School at the intersection of Bell Road and Powhatan Lakes Road, including Ivory Morris and his future wife, Clara Carrington, granddaughter of Charles Hazel (soldier) and Martha Hazel (nurse), a biracial couple who met during the Civil War and led a lifelong struggle against racism and social injustices. Early Mohemenco teachers were parents of the students, including Annie (Bell) Morris, Henrietta (Bell) Taylor, and Thaddeus Hewitt.

Sixty-one years after James's death, his grandsons Ivory, James, John (Belmead and Saint Francis employees) and other parents petitioned the court to integrate the Powhatan Public Schools. In 1963, sixty-five African American students integrated the Powhatan County

Public Schools. The first African American graduate of Powhatan High School was James's great-granddaughter, Sandra Rose (Morris) Kemp, who also became the first African American to graduate from Virginia Commonwealth University School of Fashion Design. Kemp continued the Morris family's long association with the fields of agriculture and education at three land-grant universities. After graduating from the University of the District of Columbia in adult education and the University of Maryland School of Agriculture with training in extension/rural education, Kemp became the first African American to serve as a USDA/Colorado State University 4-H extension agent/clothing and textiles resource person for the seven-county High Plains District in Kiowa County, Colorado.

Kemp's most memorable extension experience occurred when she and her secretary, Velda Benner, returned from a twelve-hour exhibit day activity. As they approached the Sand Creek massacre area in Chivington, the car went out of control and came to rest in a plowed corn field. The automobile mechanic said the belts broke and became entangled. Kemp and Benner believed that they had experienced the "revenge of the Cheyennes."

Several of James's great-granddaughters graduated from Saint Francis de Sales School. Sandra Morris Kemp has represented the Morris family on Francis/Emma Inc. Board of Directors and Advisory Committee and Belmead Granary Restoration Planning Circle (excerpt from *Slavery to Freedom: An African American Family's Documented Sojourn* (2004) by Sandra Kemp).

CHAPTER 5

Mohemenco Hamlet, African American Public Education, and Civil Rights in Powhatan, Virginia

On Bell Road (Route 684), a historical marker highlights the Mohemenco community and the eras of slavery, reconstruction, segregation, and integration through people living during these eras in Mohemenco. (It reads: Mohemenco [a Monacan village] and Drake House. Colonel Samuel Drake [1787–1863], justice of the peace, coroner, inn owner, militiaman, son of James Drake [1740–1796, Revolutionary War soldier, Methodist minister, and blacksmith of Little Deep Creek] owned 1,048 acres, including Caxamalka Plantation and 18 slaves. In 1879 Martha Wood [1843–1920], Drake's mulatto ex- slave/nurse appeared in court for violating miscegenation laws. Her ancestors were Bamileke people of Cameroon, West Africa. In 1882, Frank Falcon, Belmead freedman/sharecropper, acquired 10 acres including Drake House [built in 1822]. Sold to Edmonia Harden Booker, Mohemenco Colored School cook [1943], then to Sandra Morris Kemp [2004], first African American graduate of Powhatan High School, Martha Wood's great-granddaughter.) Sandra Kemp provided the research information. The Michaux-St. James Foundation erected the marker with funding from the foundation and Sandra Kemp.

Mohemenco Hamlet is located in Macon Magisterial District in Powhatan, Virginia. It encompasses the rural area between Route 60 and Cartersville/Cosby Roads south and north and Powhatan Lakes Road and Howell Road east and west. Route 621 (Cosby Road) was named Mohemenco Road on the Virginia Historical Inventory map in 1937.

Historically, the word *Mohemenco* is associated with the Monacan Indians who were of the Siouan tribe and controlled the area between the fall line in Richmond and the Blue Ridge Mountains. They were enemies of the Powhatan Confederacy (Tribes). The five villages were Massinacak and Mowhemenchough or Mowhemencho in Powhatan, Rassawek near the Rivanna River, Monahassanugh near Wingina, and Monasukapanough near Charlottesville. The French Huguenots renamed the former site of Mowhemencho to Manikin-Town. By the early 1700s, the Monacans had disappeared from the area.

European Landowners

During slavery, European landowners with the names of Taylor, Hobson, Drake, and Cocke occupied the Mohemenco area. Their plantations were named Ashland, Mount Hope, Brookland, Woodlawn, Caxamalka, Beldale, and Belmead. Remnants of this history in Mohemenco include Peterville Church and Cemetery. (Peterville is Located 2.1 miles west of Powhatan on Route 60 and .2 miles northeast on a private road to the church.) The church is dated 1802. The first church was built and supported by the crown. This church was rebuilt and deeded by William Mayo to the following trustees, Littlebury Moseby, William Hickman, Thomas Miller, Miceleburg Montague, Josiah Smith in 1802. These trustees of the Episcopal Church stipulated that no Negro was to ever preach there, and preference must be given Episcopal ministers. This building was burned, and in 1854, William D. Taylor deeded the land on which a new brick church was built and called Peterville by the Baptist. The trustees were James R. Eggleston and John Liggon. The Baptists are the present owners. The present Peterville Church is a large brick building set back from the highway in woods. The grounds have grown up as no services are held there now. It is a very plain building with double doors in front and a single door on the east side. The pulpit is small, almost square, and about eight inches from the floor The simple balcony extends on three sides. The pews have been sold.

The site for the original church was chosen by Pierre Legrand "Dis place vieldo." He was prominent in colonial affairs, being at one time a member of the House of Burgess and afterward revolutionary statesman and a leading figure in the convention which formed the new United States of America. The church was named *Pierreville*. It was built and supported by the crown. After the Revolutionary War, the church property was sold for the benefit of the public. The church had fallen into disrepair and had been used as barracks or stables in many cases. The present building was erected by the Baptist and is slightly to the north of the site of the second Peterville Church, which was burned.

Ministers were very scarce and served a very large territory with only occasional services in each church. The first minister recorded seems to have been Reverend John Robinson in 1751. Then Reverend McLaurin was rector until his death in 1772. He was buried under the floor of the chancel of the old church. In 1772, Reverend Alexander MacRae was rector. He was a Scotchman and did not enter into the spirit of the times of the American Revolution and was warned to leave. He disregarded the warning, so one night a messenger told him that a dying neighbor wanted to see him. He was waylaid and led to a tree, where he was whipped. The tree has long been cut down but was known as the "Parson's Pine." A petition was sent to Williamsburg to have him banished, but Patrick Henry added his influence to another petition to have him retained. One of the signers of the petition to keep him was Bennett Goode. (Bennett Good Tract was named "Forest Home." It was inherited from Bennett Goode by John Goode. John left it to his daughter Emily Goode Taurman. She gave it to her son, Henry E. Taurman. Henry's daughter, Hallie Taurman Hepgood, inherited the home. There are brick chimneys to the present house built by Mr. Harrison, who was the son of the Harrison who fought at the Battle of Waterloo. John Goode was in the Revolutionary War and also present at Yorktown. Bennett Goode was the brother-in-law of Lieutenant Samuel Watkins, an officer in the Revolutionary War. A monument was erected in memory of Watkins by the Frances Bland Randolph Chapter of the Daughters of the American Revolution in 1928 at the old Peterville Church.) From 1789, Reverend Hopkins served here until his death in 1807. Then Reverend William Lee served until 1826. After the Baptist rebuilt the church, Reverend Hardy Harrison preached here for some time. The church has not been used for regular services in some time.[35]

Adjacent to the Peterville Church site is the cemetery, located on the north side of Route 60, one-eighth mile east of Bell Road on the other side of the pond (Harris's).

Other cemeteries include the Lawson, Taylor (Ashland), and the Drake Cemetery. (This cemetery has a single tombstone which reads: "In memory of Terressa Ann Wiley, wife of F. M. Wiley of Fincastle and daughter of Thomas and Terressa Drake, born 17th October 1820, died 19th September 1841. In her were centered all that a devoted husband, loving mother, brothers, sisters, and relatives could desire.")

The plat for the James Drake's estate of 344 acres, surveyed by William Clarke in 1805, shows a school located south of John Howard's tract, north of Molly Drake's tract, east of Robert Taylor's tract, and west of Howard Creek (Geddes Creek). It also shows the manor house of James and Molly Drake. In 1796, James Drake advertised in the *Virginia Gazette* and *General Advertiser* for a runaway from his plantation in Mohemenco. (It reads: $30.00 for returning or $15.00 for securing in jail a mulatto Negro by the name of Sam (born 1769), 6 feet, 27 years old, a shoemaker, cooper, shingle getter, and sawyer who has gone to South Carolina to be with his wife.) At his death in 1796, James's inventory included the following slaves: Shadrack, Morecco, George, Stephen, Charles, Margaret, Pheba, Charlotte, Phillis, Maria, Harry, and Pat. Molly's inventory of slaves at her death in 1828 included George, Sepio, Dinah, Caroline, Janey, and Peter. The estate of James Drake also contained 228 acres on Buckingham Road near Powhatan Courthouse.

[35.] Works Progress Administration of Virginia, Historical Inventory, 1936 and 1937. (Peterville Church). http://image.lva.virginia.gov/VHI/html/21/0561.html

Other historical homes include Provost (Oakville), Taylor's Seat (Hard Scrabble)/Rosemont, and Travelers' Rest. (It was located 0.1 mile east of Provost, Virginia, on Route 16, then 0.1 mile west on a private road.) The home was built in 1788. Owners were Robert Taylor, Blagrave Taylor, Oswell B. Taylor, Sam Palmore, and Leo Carpenter (African American, graduate of St. Emma's, and instructor in the Trades Department at St Emma's). Travelers' Rest comes up to its name: such a sweet restful place. Now the weeds are very high. The house is being repaired and will be an attractive home. It has one very large chimney in the center of the house about ten feet square, and the bottom part is made of rock. There are four fireplaces to the one chimney. This home has six rooms. It has six panel Christian cross doors put together with wooden pegs. Part of the doors have H hinges and part have modern hinges. The original house had one porch, Colonial style. Now there are three porches: one on the back and two small ones on the front. Robert Taylor was a successful farmer and owned many acres of land. To his son Blagrave, he gave Travelers' Rest. Blagrave trained for duty in the war between the states in Major W. S. Dance's battery but died before he saw actual service. His wife, Amanda Taylor, had quite a hard time (as many others did). She had to sell her carriage and ride in a wagon. She made suits for the Cocke family. Mrs. Cocke wanted to adopt the youngest child of the Taylor family, but Mrs. Taylor would not give her consent. Shortly afterward, the child died. During the war, Mrs. Taylor was so easily frightened she closed her home and came to Powhatan, Virginia, to live.[36]

Blagrave Taylor had a shoe shop and made shoes before the War between the States. Mr. Taylor also made wooden spectacle frames.

African Americans

During Reconstruction and after, freedmen sharecropped on the former plantations and later purchased land from these estates

---

[36.] Works Progress Administration of Virginia, Historical Inventory, 1937. (Traveler's Rest). http://image.lva.virginia.gov/VHI/html/21/0709.

and settled with their families in Mohemenco. Many freedmen were skilled laborers—carpenters, millers, and stonemasons on the plantations. They built homes, churches, and schools and operated businesses. Most were farmers and supplemented their income by work at the nearby Belmead Farm and St. Emma's and St. Francis de Sales Schools as tradesmen, teachers, maintenance men, agricultural workers, and domestics. Some worked at local dairy farms.

The lumber industry was another source of employment for African American men. A timber contractor from the area had a large timber tract near Toano, Virginia. He hired men from Cartersville, Tamworth-James Town, and Mohemenco to work at a lumber camp. They were transported from the area on a truck that had a flatbed converted into a rough camper. It had benches on both sides and a woodstove in the middle, with a chimney protruding from the top of the camper. The timber campsite was a couple of hours away. The group left at five thirty on Monday morning and returned on Friday afternoon. The men, after being away from their families for a week and performing dangerous work, returned for a weekend of socializing and relaxing at local taverns—drinking, dancing, etc. Some men worked as carpenters and lumber workers at several lumberyards in the county. Others were self-employed as pulp woodcutters. Some worked for the railroad part-time. Another group constructed stills and engaged in moonshining: the illegal distillation of alcoholic liquors. Some worked at the Naval Ship Yard in Tidewater, Virginia.

In the late '50s and '60s, some of the women of Mohemenco began to work outside of the home. They worked in Bon Air and other Richmond suburban areas as domestics. Some drove themselves; others were part of a carpool. A few lived on the lot and came home on the weekend by way of the Trailways/Greyhound bus.

In the late 1800s and early 1900s, many went north seeking employment opportunities. The freedmen did not sell their land. They kept the land in the family. Many of the descendants of these freedmen now live in Mohemenco or own land in Mohemenco. Many return to Mohemenco upon retirement from jobs in the north. An effort is underway to save the land of their ancestors. Unfortunately, thirty acres recently (2013) were lost to the heirs of one of the original settlers (Isham Hazel) of Mohemenco through a questionable adverse possession case. African American family surnames from the early settlement of Mohemenco include Morris, Mayo-Farris, Taylor, Drew, Sturdivant, Falcon, Nichols, Simms, Hobson, Hewitt, Howell, Brown, Booker, Walton, Waldron, Johnson, Bolling, Pryor, Flowers, Galagos, Wood, Logan, Harden, Bell, Hazel, Carrington, Harris, Venable, Scott, Seay, Ligon, Ransome, Royal, Lynch, Hudson, Vaughan, Jackson, Braxton, Thomas, Williams, Turpin, James, Elridge, Goode, Ford, Mosby, Swann, Tucker, and White.

Three Letters Survive from the Early 1900s

February 17, 1937, letter from Reverend William Simms of Powhatan, Virginia, to the Virginia State Board of Education, Richmond, Virginia. He is complaining about Powhatan County's promise to build a modern high school for Negro children with light, heat, and plumbing facilities on a piece of land purchased, payed for, and deeded to the county by the colored citizens, in addition to $3,000 raised to help pay for the facility by the colored community. He is asking for state assistance in construction of the promised facility. The letter is signed by Reverend Simms and several trade instructors from Belmead.

August 6, 1927, reply letter from a Mohemenco resident (signature missing) to mulatto Ruby (Farris-Mayo) Weaver, former resident of Mohemenco, now living in Pennsylvania. The letter answers Ruby's question about her deceased white father, Morris Farris, and the handling of his burial. The letter also contains information about happenings in the community. The letter was provided by Ruby's son, Albert Weaver. He dropped out of school at the age of sixteen and worked as a cleaner in a dental office. Later he took advantage of the various government executive orders that allowed him to "find a decent job." He rose to middle-management level in the Army Corps of Engineers.

September 8, 1937, letter from Annie Jane (Bell) Morris to her son, Ivory Morris, who is working in New York City as a porter/elevator operator for an apartment building near Columbia University. His address is 2700 Eighth Avenue, New York, New York. She complained about the fact that he had not written to her for several months. She informed him of the local activities in Powhatan and the status of his crop, livestock, dogs, etc.

African American Religious, Cultural, Recreational, Social, and Fraternal Activities

African American religious, cultural, recreational, social, and fraternal activities in Mohemenco included church revivals, church services, Bible studies, Sunday schools, including special programs at Easter and Christmas with gifts, fruits and candies for each child, annual Sunday school trips to segregated Buckroe Beach in Tidewater area and Prince Edward Lake (now Twin Lakes State Park) with scheduled rest stops at black businesses along the route, and summer Bible Schools, baptisms at local ponds and confirmation Sunday; family reunions; school reunions; Belmead band concerts, military drills, and vacation Bible Schools; membership in the NAACP, Mason/Order of Eastern Star, James River Baptist Association, Aid's Society (benevolent), and Elks (IBPOEW, Improved Benevolent Protective Order of the Elks of the World for blacks); and participation in the African American Powhatan County Fair and Cooperative Extension Service activities (youth and adult); women and men baseball teams; hunt clubs; boating/ fishing in the Morris, Harris (I was baptized at this pond and joined Mount Zion Church at age twelve), and Belmead Ponds, Deep Creek, Powhatan Lakes, the James River, and tidewater deep-sea fishing on rental boats. For most of the men and some women, the most enjoyable weekend activity was watching or listening to baseball games (Dodgers and Yankees/World Series.)

The Mohemenco Community's Medical Needs

The Mohemenco community's medical needs were met by doctors, midwives, and individuals skilled in home remedies. Dr. James Tilman of Rock Castle was the physician for St. Emma's and St. Francis de Sales Schools. He also delivered babies and carried for the sick. In 1912, Dr. Tilman referred my father to an eye doctor in Richmond. At age six, Ivory Morris crossed the James River on the Belmead Ferry and rode the train for the first time. Other doctors who provided services to patients in Mohemenco were Dr. Henning (Mohemenco Road, now Cosby Road), Dr. Snead (Cartersville), Dr. Lloyd (Maidens), Dr. Robert Bradley (Powhatan Village), and Dr. Bowles (African American) of Sandy Hook, Goochland, Virginia. African American midwives included Henrietta Strange Morris, Marylee Brown Taylor, Ms. Sturdivant, and Annie Brown Minor Palmore. Cousin Annie delivered white and black babies. She made her home in Cumberland. Her husband Richard "Dick" Palmore was a barber. He only cut hair for white clients. Home remedies and health practices included the wearing of undershirts from October to May regardless of the temperature, a drop of turpentine/kerosene on a teaspoon of sugar for congestion, cod liver's oil and Scott's emulsion and Castoria (castor oil) for cleansing. These items were purchased from the traveling Raleigh man, Belmead Store, Maxey's Store (Village), Pleasant's Store (Cartersville), Nichol's Store (Macon), Sledd's Store (Route 60), and A. G. Smith (Maidens).

The African American Community of Mohemenco Included Churches, Cemeteries, Schools, Historical Homes, and Businesses

Mohemenco Churches and Cemeteries

History indicates that some African Americans of Mohemenco attended services with their masters during slavery and sat in the back or in the balcony of the church. Philip St. George Cocke constructed a *slave chapel* for his slaves with a white Baptist minister conducting the services. Some slaves attended *Muddy Creek Baptist Church*. The slave masters of Mohemenco attended Emmanuel Episcopal Church near the Powhatan Village. African Americans and whites attended *Peterville Church (St. James Parish Vestry)*. After slavery, freedman James Thomas (an ex-slave of Belmead) and his wife, Maria, held weekly prayer services in their home. Between 1888 and 1889, this group organized and established the Colored Baptist Church. The organizers were James Thomas, Maria Thomas, T. J. Venable, Dawson Brown, Sr., Robert Walton, John Walton, and Reverend Alfred Goodwyn. Greenbrier's original church was built on James Thomas's ten-acre tract purchased from the Williams's Plantation on Route 621 in 1865. Issac Waldron, contractor, built the Colored Baptist Church on the one-acre tract deeded to the trustees on September 6, 1890. The church is located high upon a hill near a stream. Later the church became known as *Greenbrier Baptist Church*.

In 1909, the second cemetery was started, located east of the original church site. The three-fourth-acre tract of land was deeded October 31, 1913, to the church as a burial site by Captain Joseph Hobson of Brookland Plantation, Confederate officer in the Powhatan troop who was hospitalized at Huguenot Springs Hospital. It is rumored that Martha Wood (my great-grandmother) met Charles Hazel, white soldier, at the same hospital while caring for Captain Hobson. Her parents were slaves on the Brookland Plantation. The cemetery remained in use until October 10, 1956. There are eleven graves in the original churchyard. There are seventy-one graves, and thirty-nine are unmarked in the second cemetery. My ancestors Wood, Hazel, and Carrington are interred in this cemetery.

Ministers include Reverends Alfred Goodwyn, Robert Turner, John Jordan, William Simms, Phillip Cook, James Jefferson, Ross, and Delmar Wright. Other churches associated with Mohemenco residents included Mount Zion, Little Zion, Hollywood, and Antioch Baptist Churches (Reverend Alfred Morris founded Mount Zion Baptist Church in 1872 and served as pastor at the three other churches). Alfred Morris (1816–1882) was a stonemason on the Belmead Plantation of antebellum landowner Philip St. George

Cocke. Mount Zion is located off Route 60 on Ridge Road. Alfred's property was next to the property of James Morris in Mohemenco.

In 1925, 1.5 acres of land was purchased on Bell Road from George W. Brown to build a new church. John Bell Sr., contractor, built the present church in 1928. The church purchased a piece of land adjacent to the church property line to be used as a cemetery site and is in use today. All that remains of the old church are the foundation piers and concrete steps. In cemetery 2 of the old church is the burial site of a white Confederate soldier, Isham Hazel. He was married to a woman of color, Martha Wood. Martha shared ancestry with the Bamileke, Hausa (Nigerian), and Tikar—peoples of Cameroon, Western Africa. He died in 1915. His son-in-law Paulus Carrington (died in 1916 when struck by lightning and left ten children) is also buried in this cemetery. Isham's and Paulus's tracts of land were on the extension of Powhatan Lakes Road that formerly continued to Cosby Road (Mohemenco Road) near the original Greenbrier Church.

Other African American cemeteries are on family land, including Etta Taylor, Howell Road; Hall, Hewitt, and Ligon on Powhatan Lakes Road; and James Morris, Mosby, Brown, and Drew (burial site of African American Tyler Drew, Confederate soldier) off of Bell Road. The Belmead Historical Cemetery and Catholic cemetery include slaves, ex-slaves, and Protestant employees and Catholics from the Mohemenco area.

Mohemenco Schools

Schools—in 1887, Tyler Drew (1843–?), freedman of Belmead Plantation and his wife, Mary, deeded land for the Mohemenco Colored Community School. The building was also used for Greebrier Baptist Church activities. The school was located on the northwest corner at the intersection of Bell Road and Powhatan Lakes Road. The school had two rooms and seven grades. The early students were taught the 3Rs and catechism. Early teachers were parents of the students. Later teachers were graduates of training schools. A cook provided a lunch of soup. The school was heated by a woodstove. The students walked to school. A number of African American students attended St. Emma's Parochial School (1897–1938). This school was for children of Saint Francis de Sales and St. Emma's employees. It was located in the old Cocke's Slave Chapel. A few Catholic children of Mohemenco attended Holy Providence in Pennsylvania. Later colored community schools in the county were closed and consolidated into a central elementary school, Pocahontas, on Route 60. Teachers from the Mohemenco area or teachers at Mohemenco include Virginia Sturdivant, Christianna V. Waldron, Hettie (Finney) Hewitt, Ms. Cheatam, Parthenia (Drew) Wood Morris, Mildred (Taylor) Morris, Gae (Hall) Waldron Peterson, Belle (Taylor) Matthews, Mattie (Bell) West, Blanche (Hewitt) Canada, Hattie (Criss) Wood, Mozelle Swann, Octavia (Harris) Lewis, Arnetha (Hobson) Hobson, Jennie (Parker) Brown Taylor Bell, William Wood, and James Venable. Belmead trades instructors from Mohemenco include Lewis Dixon, Leo Carpenter, Ivory Morris, Winfred Taylor, Lonnie Bell, Velon Bell, John Morris, George Morris, Robinson Taylor, Willie Sturdivant, Douglas Royall, Everette Hobson, and Moses Taylor.

To end a segregated school system, the case of *Edwin Alvin Bell et. al. v. Powhatan County School Board* was submitted to the courts. The decision allowed sixty-five African American elementary and high school students to integrate the former all-white schools in 1963. The majority of the students were from the Mohemenco community. The first African American graduate of Powhatan High School in 1965 was a Mohemenco resident: Sandra Rose Morris. African Americans from Mohemenco Hamlet were involved in the Powhatan County, Virginia, education and civil rights movement for equality.

Mohemenco Historical Homes

Homes—Mohemenco had several historical homes that were associated with the African American community:

- *James and Jane Morris's home* is located in Mohemenco Hamlet, Macon District, about half a mile from Belmead property. It consists of a fifty-four-acre tract. A family cemetery and "Ashland" cemetery, a pond, and two houses are on the property. It is bound on the north and east by Route 684, south by Route 625, and west by Route 637. The two-story house of James Morris had a kitchen and a dining room on one side and a vestibule on the first floor. The bedrooms were upstairs. His two sons, George and Willie, remodeled and expanded the house and lived there with their families. In 1914, George built a two-story home on the property east of the James Morris house. James's house has fallen. George's house was remodeled to a one-story house.

- *Travelers' Rest* is on the west side of Bell Road and south of Provost when traveling north. It was the home of Robert Taylor (1788 to 1811), Blagrave Taylor (1811 to 18——), Oswell B. Taylor (1861 to 1915), Sam Palmore (1915 to 1932), and African American Leo Carpenter and his heirs from 1932 to the present. Leo graduated from St. Emma's and taught in the trades department at St. Emma's. A second story was added to the house. It is now in disrepair.

- *Dr. James Tilman's home* is on the east side of Bell Road and south of the site of the defunct Waldron Store. It is a two-story with a front porch. Dr. Tilman was the physician for the St. Emma's and St. Francis de Sales Schools. African Americans Martin and Eliza (Wood) Peterson purchased the house. It was later sold to African Americans George Ransome (Pocahontas High School principal) and Alberta Ransome (teacher). It is now owned by their heirs. The Drake Historical Cemetery lies at the back of the property.

- *Tyler and Ellen Bell's home* is located on the west side of Bell Road and south of Stegers Creek when traveling north. Tyler was a slave on the Bell Plantation, North Carolina, along with his father, John; mother, Jane; and siblings. His family was relocated to the Jeters Plantation in Jetersville, Amelia, Virginia. After slavery, Tyler and his family took the surname of their former master. They preferred Bell to Jeters. Ellen was a slave in Trenholm, Virginia, and was associated with the Parker family. Records list her as Ellen (Marion/Scott) Robinson. Family history records her as Ellen Parker. Her mother was Anne Archer Robinson, and her grandmother was Charity Robinson. Anne married Jim Hatcher. Tyler and Ellen raised four sons and five daughters on the land they purchased from the Taylor tract. Cartersville/Belmead Road was renamed to Bell during the late twentieth century. To the south of the house is the Bell Pavilion that honors the contributions of Tyler, Ellen, and their descendants.

- *Lee and Suzy (Hobson) Wood's home* is at the end of the current Powhatan Lakes Road (east), east of Bell Road, west of Geddes Creek, north of Falcon House, and south of Cosby Road. (Earlier, Powhatan Lakes Road continued on the property to Cosby Road.) Lee Wood was the son of Washington and Mary Wood, slaves on the Hobson plantation. Lee purchased his tract of land from the Samuel Drake's estate, built his home, and farmed the land. His son Arthur inherited the land and lived in the house. During the late twentieth century, the house and land were sold. The house is a one-story building painted blue.

- *Frank and Alice (Hobson) Falcon's home* is located on the west side of Powhatan Lakes Road (east), east of Bell Road, south of old Hobson Road/old Greenbrier Church, west of Geddes Creek, and north of Stegers Creek. Frank Falcon was a freedman from Belmead Plantation and one of the founders of Mount Zion Baptist Church. He acquired in 1882 a ten-acre tract and house (built in 1822) from the Samuel Drake estate. The two-story center-passage building had a tall exterior chimney at each end. The foundation was stone piers. The roof was covered with slate shingles. The house fell in 2009. A picture of the house appears on the "Mohemenco and Drake House" historical marker on Bell Road.

African American Businesses and
Tradesmen of Mohemenco

African American businesses and tradesmen of Mohemenco. Historically, employment opportunities for the African Americans were limited in county, state, and federal governments and private industry. Many African American were farmers, self-employed tradesmen, or menial laborers. A few worked in professional positions (educators and preachers) or operated businesses. During the days of segregation, these individuals were productive members of society and were excellent role models for the community. A number of individuals operated stores, including Johnny and Alberta (Hobson) Harris at the intersection of Route 60 (south side) and Bell Road, Robert and Alice (Drew) Hobson (defunct) ("Hobson-Harris") at the intersection of Bell Road and Powhatan Lakes Road, Frank and Gae (Hall) Waldron (defunct) on Bell Road, William Walton on Bell Road, and William and Shirley (Morris) Walton's Store and Restaurant (defunct) at the intersection of Bell Road (east side) and Route 60 (north side), and Walton's Funeral Home (Route 60). Three post offices operated in the community, one at the residence of Andrew and Ellen (Hall) Brown on Bell Road, the second at Provost, and the third at Rock Castle (a rower in a boat transported the mail across the James River.)

Tradesmen

- Douglas and Archibald Royal, electricians
- George Morris, carpenter, mechanic, and flat/ferry builder
- John Howell, veterinarian
- Louis Dixon, carpenter
- Leo Carpenter, plumber
- Ivory Morris, carpenter and ferry builder
- Winfred Taylor, woodworking
- John Morris, plumber
- Velon Bell, automobile mechanic
- Lonnie Bell, ironworking
- John Bell, Sr., building contractor

- Issac Waldron, building contractor
- John Hobson, carpenter
- James Morris, miller and carpenter
- Charleston Taylor, carpenter
- Robinson Taylor, wheelwright
- Alfred Morris, stonemason and Minister of the Gospel and circuit minister for First Antioch, Little Zion, Mount Zion, and Hollywood Baptist churches

Ministers E. T. Jefferson and Theolophilus P. Harris performed marriage ceremonies for Mohemenco couples. Andrew Jasper and Dan Watson (Maidens area) operated "stores on wheels" throughout the hamlet of Mohemenco.

African American Public Education and Civil Rights in Powhatan, Virginia

Community Schools—First to Seventh Grades

In *Plessy v. Ferguson* (1896), the Supreme Court of the United States ruled that "separate but equal" accommodations were constitutional, and segregation became a way of life. By 1880, a school tax of ten cents was levied on county personal and real property. The county operated two school systems—one white and one black. The colored community schools began around the early 1900s and usually were one- or two-rooms schools located on the property of Baptist churches. The early students were taught the 3Rs and catechism in grades 1 through 4. Later, grades were 5 through 7 and included more subjects to the curriculum. Early teachers were parents of the students and graduates of training schools. A cook provided a lunch of soup or sandwiches. The school was heated by a woodstove. The students walked to school.

Parents had a say in the erection and placing of the building. Some donated land for building the local schools. On January 2, 1888, Tyler Drew (Freedman from Belmead plantation) and his wife donated one acre of land in Macon District at the intersection of Bell Road and Powhatan Lakes Road for the Public Free School or the Mohemenco Colored Community School (1897–1950s). The building was used for Greenbrier Church services. The Sunday school of Greenbrier was organized here. Some schools would be known as the Rosenwald Schools because of the foundation's major financial contribution for education in the south. One such school was the Tamworth School or Little Zion School on Cartersville Road. In 1938 or as early as 1925, a one-room schoolhouse was built next to Little Zion Church. On Saturday evenings, slide shows were held for the students, and home-made ice cream was sold as a fund-raiser. Charles Franklin Simpson served as the supervisor for colored schools for the county of Powhatan.

The colored community schools included Ballsville Black School, Buckingham Road (with teacher Sadie Hopkins-Green); Pilkinton School (teacher Sally Tyler); Pine Hill, Worsham Road (teachers Fanny Finny, Norvella Finney-Ambrose, and Mattie Bell West); Hollywood Community School, Buckingham Road (with lower grades at the Fair Building [1920] destroyed by fire in 1928, rebuilt in 1929); Union Branch Elementary; Antioch School, Maidens Road (teacher Octavia H. Lewis); Macon Black School, Giles Bridge Road (teachers Mattie West and Novella Ambrose); Shiloh School, intersection of 617 and 633 (teacher Mozelle Swann); Loganville, Ballsville Road (teacher Lillie Simpson); Little Zion, Cartersville Road (teachers Mozelle Swann, Reverend Perkins, Celestine Simpson Jordan, William Douglas Drew, Mariah Drew, Minnie Thompson, Lillie Simpson, Blanche Hewitt Canada, and Charles Simpson); Dorset School; and Mohemenco Colored School, intersection of Bell and Powhatan Lakes Road (teachers C. V. Waldron, Hattie Criss, Mozelle Swann, Belle Taylor Matthews, and Hettie Finney-Hewitt).

Centralized Elementary Education— First to Seventh Grades

Before 1930s, no black high school was in Powhatan. Some grad-uates of the community school continued their education at Maggie

Walker or Armstrong High Schools in Richmond by relocating and living with relatives in the city. After the 1930s, the graduates of the community schools continued their education at Powhatan Training School. Around 1950s, colored community schools in the county were closed and consolidated into a central elementary school, Pocahontas Elementary School on Route 60. Funds were appropriated to build a brick elementary school next to the brick Pocahontas High School. The students studied geography, reading, writing, arithmetic, spelling, history, English, and music (in the high school auditorium).

There were two teachers per grade for the first through the fifth grades: for first grade, there were Sadie Green and Novella F. Ambrose; second grade, Gae Waldron and Celestine Jordan; third grade, Mattie West and Lillie Simpson/Corrine Langley; fourth grade, Belle Matthews and Octavia Lewis; fifth grade, Sally Tyler and Jennie Hopkins. The sixth and seventh grades had three teachers: Hattie Criss, Blanche Canada, and Mozelle Swann. Each of the three rooms housed both sixth and seventh grade students. Other teachers included Sarah Gordon, Ms. Shipp, Ms. Crenshaw, Ms. Johnson, Cynthia Canady Walker, and Annie Howell. The first through the third grades were on the lower level and contained bathrooms and coatrooms in the back of the classrooms. The fourth through the seventh grades were on the upper level and had hall bathrooms.

Rosa L. Martin's office was on the upper level with pictures of boxer Joe Louis and Singer Marian Anderson on the wall. She served as principal for the elementary school and supervisor of colored schools. The outer office served as a teacher's supply room with a mimeograph machine. A cafeteria and snack area were located in the back of the elementary school and served high school and elementary students. Virginia Hewitt, Margaret Harris, and Addie Green were the cafeteria workers. The playground was to the west of the building. Emory Finney and Frank Jasper were the maintenance men. Mr. Finney also served as a school bus driver. Activities included Friday-afternoon hobby period, May Day, elementary graduation, after school private piano lessons/visits to Finney's store, plays, music, movies, class fund-raising (Wise potato chips and Hershey bars), and trips to historical sites, including the county and state fairs.

Secondary Education—Eighth to Twelfth Grades

Following improvements to the white schools, black parents requested funds in April 1932 for the building of a black high school to the board of supervisors. In October 1936, blacks were told that a two-room school for blacks in Huguenot District would be built with funds borrowed from the Literacy Fund. In December 1936, the Public Works Administration authorized funds to build a school for blacks, along with funds from a loan from the State Literacy Fund. By 1939, the Black High School was completed. Local blacks contributed $3,000, including the James River District Baptist Association/the Women's Missionary and Educational Convention. Also, a two-room black school in Huguenot and a one-room school in Macon were built. The school year expanded from eight months to nine months. In 1941, the school board and the board of supervisors considered a home economics cottage, dental clinic (white and black), technological and agricultural building, and school buses for black children. In 1944, funds were appropriated for the erection of a cannery on the grounds of Powhatan County Colored School. In 1948, the school board added new classrooms to Powhatan and Pocahontas High Schools. Eight new classrooms were added to each school, as well as equipment and transportation through a bond referendum. In 1937, a loan from the Literacy Fund was approved to construct a new agricultural building at Pocahontas High School and a two-room addition to the high school and a two-room addition for the elementary school.

There were three colored high schools: The Powhatan Training School (1931–1937) was located across from Hollywood Baptist Church at the junction of Route 13 and Route 60 (site of VDOT). In 1932, the first graduating class consisted of four students. The principals were Ms. Mary Price (1931–1932), Reverend J. H. Coles (1932–1933), Mr. Edwards (1933–1934), and in 1934, George Ransome became the fourth principal. In 1937, the Powhatan Training School was renamed Powhatan Colored High School (1937–1942). George Ransome continued as principal. Powhatan Colored High School changed its name to Pocahontas High School in 1942 and continued under that name until the two county high schools were fully consolidated in 1969. Later Powhatan High School became the Village Building, and Powhatan Elementary School became the Social Services Building. Pocahontas Elementary and High Schools became the Pocahontas Middle School. The integrated school system consists of five schools (Pocahontas Elementary, Flat Rock Elementary, Powhatan Elementary, Pocahontas Middle School, and Powhatan High School). George Ransome continued as principal until 1967. James B. Venable served as principal from 1967 to 1969.

There was no graduating class in 1951 because in 1951, a twelfth grade was added to Pocahontas High School. The 1952 graduating class completed twelve years of study. Starting in 1952, the graduating classes began electing class officers: president/vice president, secretary/assistant secretary, and treasurer. High school consisted of five grades (8–12).

During the '60s, there were two eighth-grade homerooms and one homeroom for each freshman, sophomore, junior, and senior class. At the back of the high school were the home economics cottage and the agricultural building. The auditorium was located in the high school, and it was used by the elementary and high school for assemblies and graduations. The sports areas were to the east of the building: baseball diamond, basketball court, and softball/physical education field. Around 1960, a science laboratory and library were added to the west side of the high school.

The subjects offered included English and literature, mathematics and algebra, history, science, biology, agriculture, home economics, government, business, and later a foreign language. Teachers included Monroe Hite, Ms. R. Stafford, Mrs. Lazenby, Ms. Burns, Ms. Rankins, James Venable, George Ransome, Freddye Finney, Edward Finney, Mary Finney, Carolyn (Mumford) Harris, Bessie (Holloman) Bell, Ms. Prescott, and Librarian Geraldyne Scott.

School activities included FHA, FFA, chorus, movies, dances, student council, county and state fair trips, proms, junior and senior trips, honor roll assemblies, observation of Black History Week, softball, baseball, basketball, May Day, elementary and high school graduations, and science competitions. A display of sports and science competition awards was in the hallway.

Civil Rights

In May 1954, the Supreme Court outlawed separate but equal facilities in public education in *Brown vs. Board of Education of Topeka*. Opposition had grown into massive resistance by the whites. Powhatan Resolution of July 24, 1954, stated: "The Board of Supervisors is opposed to the operation of non-segregated public schools and plans to use its power to ensure the continuation of a segregated school system and the budget passed on Monday, August 8, 1954 was for segregated schools only, not for the operation of any integrated school." The white-only Huguenot Academy was established as an escape from racial integration.

The black population made demands that entered the county board, school board, and court records by pushing for integration of the schools and civil rights and achieved racial equality in the following ways:

1. *Edward Alvin Bell et. al. v. County School Board of Powhatan County, Virginia and J. S. Caldwell, Division Superintendent of Schools of Powhatan, Virginia*. The complaint was filed on August 17, 1962, by twenty-six persons who were parents of sixty-five infants all being Negroes and domiciled in Powhatan County, Virginia.
2. Parents James and Alice Morris, Ivory and Clara Morris, and Douglas and Lucille Evans completed the pupil placement forms to enroll Maria Morris, Alcibia Morris, and Pauline Evans in the first grade at Powhatan White Elementary School on September 4, 1962, and earlier. All attempts failed to gain enrollment of the three children.
3. In 1963, E. D. Hobson and Clarence N. Brown, representing the "Progressive Negro Citizens," filed a list of demands to the board of supervisors: erase racial signs on the courthouse toilets, employment of Negroes in local government jobs (thirteen were enumerated), biracial committees, and information as to Negro and the War Memorial Building.

In 1963, the court allowed sixty-three students (grades 2–11) to integrate the schools, allowing for partial integration. In 1965, the first African American graduated from Powhatan High School— Sandra Rose Morris. The Public Education Committee held two biracial meetings in the summer of 1964 to have the consolidation movement on the part of the school board reversed. On December 11, 1967, the board formed a permanent biracial committee to solve some of Powhatan's racial problems. The committee had one white and one black from each of the three districts in the county. In 1969, the schools were consolidated. Equality issues continued as to the hiring and retention of African American teachers and transportation.

Sources

Oral history and interviews
Personal knowledge
County heritage and bicentennial Books
School yearbooks
Celebration programs
Church anniversary celebrations
Court cases
Minutes of the Powhatan School Board and Board of Supervisors
Research paper
February 1934 minutes of the James River Women's Missionary and
    Education Convention
February 1937 letter from Reverend William Simms and others com-
    plaining about school plan not providing for modern facilities

Miscellaneous: Photographs courtesy of author and others.

Ex-slaves Photographs
Top left: Ellen (Parker-Robinson) Bell (1856-1931)
Top middle: John Tyler Bell (1856-1943)
Top right: Richard Taylor (1844-1924)
*Center left: James "Jim" Morris (1820-1902)
Center right: Kitty (Morris) Ford (1849-1946)
*Bottom Left: Napoleon Bonapart Drew (1843-1925)
Bottom Center: Lucy Ann (Pryor) Bailey Wood (1861-1942)
Bottom right (left): Rachel (Bolling) Pryor Howell (1838-1914)
Bottom right (right): Adeline (Lynch) Bolling (1794-1896)
*Photographs courtesy Cocke and Elliot Family Papers,
UVA, Small Collection

Luther Morris and the Belmead Mail rowboat (1930s–1960s)
*Photograph courtesy of The Sisters of the Blessed Sacrament

Belmead 50 feet Ferry built in 1921 by the Belmead
carpenters, George and Ivory Morris. The ferry was recovered
by Liesfeld Construction Company in October 2017 and
displayed at Rassawek Spring Festival (June 2018). Top:
Sandra Morris Kemp *Photograph courtesy of Eve Gregory
(Virginia Foundation for Archaeological Research, Inc.)
Bottom: Passengers, students and nuns
* Photograph Courtesy of The Sisters of the Blessed Sacrament

Saint Emma's Agricultural and Industrial Institute Trades School
(1890s-1970s) and trades instructors: Ivory Morris (Carpentry),
John Morris (Plumbing), Winfred Taylor (Woodworking).
*Photograph Courtesy of The Sisters of the Blessed Sacrament

CHAPTER 6

Oral Histories from Three
Mohemenco Residents

My interest in history, cultural heritage, and genealogy began when I listened to oral histories by my grandmother, Bettie Simms, grandfather, George Morris, and my father, Ivory Morris. Bettie (1874–1965) was the daughter of Henry Brown and Willie Ann ("Parker") Carter Brown of Trenholm. George (1874–1960) was the son of James Morris and Jane (Chambers) Morris. He was born on Belmead Plantation. Ivory (1906–1999) was the son of Annie Jane (Bell) Morris and George Morris of Mohemenco.

Bettie Frances (Brown) Simms

Bettie Frances (Brown) Simms was the wife of William Simms. Simms was a tobacco farmer, railroad worker, Minister of the Gospel, befriender of the ex-offender, and a social activist. They lived on a fifty-acre tract in Mohemenco Hamlet, Macon District, Powhatan, Virginia. They raised Anna Falcon, Amanda Bartlett, Robert and John "Simms" (last name unknown), Julian Johnson, and my mother, Clara Carrington. Her father, Paulus Carrington, was struck by lightning in 1916. He left a wife, Mary (Hazel) Carrington, and ten children (nine daughters and one son). The other children went to West

Virginia, Pennsylvania, New Jersey, and New York to live with relatives. Bettie was kin to my father. I spent many hours with "Grandma Simms." She taught me embroidering skills before I entered school. She loved quilting, reading the Bible, and showing her massive collection of photographs. She gave details about each picture.

She was a great teller of stories. During the nighttime, her stories kept us in suspense and spellbound. One story was about how she and her sister-in-law Hattie Hobson had been fooled by a prisoner: the escaped prisoner had pretended that he was searching for an escapee. They spent time talking with him and feeding him. Later they found out that the man was the prisoner. They recalled that he was very nice and reminded them to secure their homes. She also told me about another escapee: a rogue bull that camped out on a hilltop between her house and the source of her daily water supply: a spring. Her young niece that she was raising knew that they were very low on drinking water. She said the child took a bucket and ran to the spring and got water for them without attracting the bull's attention! She also told me that after her husband passed, she leased her acreage to local black farmers. An incident occurred in her sight: a farmer with two horses was clearing land and removing stumps. The horses were spooked and dragged the farmer through the field. He died! With another year's leasing income, she set aside funds for my college education.

Several Mohemenco teachers boarded with my grandmother: Hattie (Criss) Wood, Ms. Cheatham, and Minnie Thompson. Ms. Criss had a long history with education in the county. She taught my father, Ivory Morris, who was born in 1906, at Mohemenco Community School. She was my sixth grade teacher at Pocahontas Elementary School in 1959. Mrs. Thompson had taught at Little Zion Community School before retiring and moving in with grandmother. She told me about her life in Richmond, Virginia, before accepting a teaching position in Powhatan. She said her father owned a livery stable in the church hill area of Richmond, Virginia. While grandmother quilted, Mrs. Thompson spent her time writing poetry and making roses from crepe paper. They affectionately referred to each other as Sis Bettie and Sis Thompson. They enjoyed sitting on the front porch working on their hobbies and engaging in conversation. I enjoyed listening to the details of the talk. Mrs. Thompson would take her daily walk to the Waldron store. At times, Grandmother and I would visit Sis Hattie and encounter her rooster, which would try to attack us.

The arrival of the mailman was a welcomed event. Grandmother received many letters from relatives and friends up north. Without her knowledge, several acquaintances up north listed her as a dependent on their tax returns. She frequently received "donations" from these individuals, but not enough to be listed as a dependent. She gave me the title of "secretary." She dictated the response for me to reply to these letters. I had access to quite a bit of family happenings. Also, Grandmother would receive many visitors on Sunday evening. She would always allow them to taste her homemade dandelion wine before leaving. She noticed that there was an increase in the young people visiting her. She suspected that the draw was her wine. She discontinued the wine, and the number decreased. She had figured out the attraction.

In response to my question about her background and a picture of an elderly woman on the master bedroom's wall, she revealed the following: "This is my mother, Willie Ann Parker Carter Brown. I had an older half-brother [born before my mother was married] named Joe Parker. He went west to fight the Indians and was killed." On another occasion, I asked her what she knew about slavery. She said that her people were from Trenholm area. Her mother and her aunts were slaves. She stated that the white Trenholm half-sisters of her mother were "mean wenches." When they became angry, they would snatch the earrings from the ears of the slaves, leaving them with bleeding ears. She continued that the black ex-slaves were forgiving—when the "poor creatures" were destitute after the war, the black half-sisters fed and cared for them.

At another time, I asked about her youth. Grandmother recalled how as a young woman, before marriage, she worked for a wealthy woman up north. She said that the couple attended many parties. The mistress had many beautiful gowns and jewelry. She continued, one evening when she thought they had departed, she dressed up like the mistress: gown, shoes, jewelry, etc. She said as she was admiring herself in the mirror, she saw a shadow in the mirror and heard a roar of laughter. Next the mistress called her husband and said, "Look at Bettie." Grandmother said she had no idea why she did this, but she wanted to fall through the floor. She continued to work for the family. These adornments of the rich must have been dazzling in comparison to the typical dress for a young woman from Mohemenco. The typical daily attire, often made by hand, consisted of bloomers, camisole, corset, petticoat, plain dress, and apron. Sunday outfits were several printed and solid dresses with lace collars and laced trimmed sleeves, cotton/rayon stockings, black leather laced/tied block heeled shoes, wool coat with a velvet collar, wool or straw hat, plain black pocketbook, white gloves, single strand of pearls, and a gold wedding band. Bettie stated that the men of that day got a thrill when women stepped over a fence and revealed their ankles. Men's workday outfits of that day consisted of overalls (or khaki shirt and pants for Belmead instructors) and Brogan shoes. The hats for work were khaki baseball or straw and felt-brimmed. Men's dress outfits were dark suits, ties, Oxford shoes, and white shirts (collars were reversed when frayed to extend the life of the shirt). A wool coat completed the outfit. When a woman lost her partner, the mourning ritual involved the wearing of black, purple, and gray outfits for a period of time before resuming the usual dress.

Her generation had its own character. A bedspread was referred to as a "counterpane," and a wardrobe was a "chifforobe." Vegetable juice was called "pot liquor" and sour milk was "clabber." Grandmother prized her guest bedroom: beautiful bed with a feather mattress, sparkling porcelain "white lady" (chamber pot), ceramic printed wash bowl, and pitcher set on a dry sink, hassock (ottoman/footstool), fireplace, and radio on which we listened to programs and the soap operas (*Ma Perkins, Art Linkletter, Arthur Godfrey, Jack Benny*, etc.). Her house had the front door opposite the back door (shotgun house design). The spacious hallway had an icebox and a sewing machine. On Sundays, we would go to the living room and listen to her Victrola. A quart jar filled with a collection of buttons served as the front doorstop. Her outside buildings were toilet, smokehouse, woodshed, tobacco barn, icehouse, etc. She had the tobacco barn burned when she learned that local youth were using it as a lover's spot. I'll always remember her advice: "A good name is worth millions." My father's advice complemented Grandmother's: "Use your mother's wit and exercise common sense." One phrase, perhaps of biblical origin, was: "Great day in the morning," meaning "Wow!" They talked about hag risings, ghosts, hants, workers of roots, conjure (witchcraft) persons, etc. These stories were fascinating.

Three times we thought someone was trying to break into the house. The bedroom doorknob started to turn. Grandmother quickly locked the door. A loud crash was heard in the area of the living room. The next morning, we discovered that William Simms's large portrait had fallen. A strange noise was heard near the front bedroom window. With a lantern, Grandmother investigated and found that a cat was in the rocking chair that was against the wall; and another time, it was a tree branch rubbing against the house. At times, individuals would drive around the house with no lights. During all these episodes, Grandmother reminded us that nothing would happen to us because she trusted in the Lord!

Grandmother Bettie had tales to tell me about her experiences living in Powhatan, Virginia, during segregated days. She told me the following: "I had gone to the village [Powhatan courthouse] to shop at the store. The policy was to serve whites then blacks. After all the whites had been served, I stepped up to the counter. I did not see any whites in the store. The clerk commented, 'Don't you see this white lady? Wait for your turn.'" Grandmother was a white-looking African American.

Our parents sheltered us from some of the racism. As youngsters, when going to the village, we were not allowed to drink from the water fountain designated "colored." We hydrated ourselves before leaving home, or a soda was purchased at a store to drink. We were not allowed to work as domestic help in white homes. It was all right for my mother to supplement the income during the days of integration so that we would have the things we needed to get ahead. They wanted a better life for us. My father encouraged us to include typing in our course choices. He saw it as a way to enter the government and avoid the trap of domestic work.

Blacks in Mohemenco found ways to avoid racism when seeking medical care. Mohemenco did not have African American doctors. Initially, doctors made home visits. Later, that practice was changed to office visits. My father chose to take us to a doctor in Amelia County (near the Appomattox River). The patients would arrive at a two-story brick house with a semicircular driveway. Service was offered according to the lineup of the cars. This doctor avoided the segregation practice of having two offices—one white and one black. Inside his office were brown bottles of medicine, along a wall behind his desk, which he dispensed. One very young local doctor would call elderly blacks by their first names, but he called elderly white patients "mister" or "missus." The blacks resentfully accepted the practice. Another practice was to refer to elderly blacks as "aunt" and "uncle." One relative in the community, tiring of this practice, asked the doctor to tell her which one of his parents was a sibling to her mother or father.

Grandmother discussed train travel for blacks during the days of segregation. She talked about the Mason-Dixon line rule. In short, blacks had to go to a black section of the train that was reserved for them when the train reached a certain point in travel. She told me about two incidents. The first incident involved a brown-skinned woman and her white-looking husband traveling from the North to the South. They were sitting together in the black section. The conductor, assuming that the man was white, ordered the man to leave the black section and go to the white section where he belonged. The woman became irate and told the conductor that the man was black. She chided him for the stupid rules that caused such a situation. The second incident involved my mother's sister. On her first visit from New York to Powhatan, Virginia, she discovered how to leave New York in the white section and not go to the black section after reaching the Mason-Dixon line (a point between Pennsylvania and Maryland). When the conductor approached her, she did not speak. After several trips with no confrontation, she realized she could keep her seat from New York to Richmond. The conductor was not sure of her race. Auntie jokingly remarked, "If I had opened my mouth, he would have known that I was black."

The most unusual story Grandmother told me was the following: "Your great grandfather, Ike Hazel, was a white Yankee Civil War soldier from New York, Pennsylvania, or Ohio who met your great grandmother Martha Wood during the Civil War. Because she took such good care of him as a nurse in one of the hospitals, he credited her with saving his life. When the war was over, he married her. This was illegal and not accepted by others in the county. Judge Thomas Miller called him to answer charge of violating Virginia's miscegenation laws. Mr. Hazel would often laugh about how he took a large stick and walked the five miles from Mohemenco to the Powhatan County Courthouse and entered the courtroom with his stick to use on the local fellows who had threatened to beat him. After the judge assured him that no one was going to harm him, he put his stick away." Older family members mentioned "captain," "boat," "ill," and "Philadelphia" as key words in the Hazel story.

I kept this story with me. Around 1971, I began to research this oral history. I found that Isham did appear in the court seven times (1879 to 1882). One time he was fined $50. After that, the case appeared to have been dropped. In 2011, I discovered that he was a white Confederate soldier from Spotsylvania County, Virginia, by the pension application he completed in 1902 in Mohemenco, Virginia. Further research revealed the names of his mother, father, siblings, and his grandparents. The family knew very little about his background except for information that appeared on censuses. His death certificate offered very limited information except verification that he was white. I also discovered that there were parcels (three) of land that he purchased and farmed after Reconstruction that belonged to the family. In 2013, through a questionable adverse possession court case, his land was taken from the family. Six years later (2019), the family is involved in a court suit to regain family property that was taken fraudulently from Charles Isham Hazel's grandson. Oral history is very important. If Grandmother Bettie hadn't revealed this information, I would not have the background to research my heritage. Looking back, I am thankful and grateful that she gave me this information and that I had a sense of appreciation for history.

George Gordon Morris

George Morris was the son of ex-slaves James Morris (Belmead carpenter and miller) and Jane Chambers of Bear Castle Plantation in Buckingham County, Virginia. These plantations were owned by the Cocke family (General John Hartwell Cocke and Philip St. George Cocke). George was born in 1874 on Belmead. He recalled his mother making ashcakes, placing dough in hot ashes in the fireplace to cook, then dusting the ash particles off before eating. George was a carpenter (left-handed) and a mechanic. Three of his grandchildren are left-handed, including me. He married Annie Jane (Bell), daughter of John Tyler and Ellen (Robinson-Parker) Bell. Before marriage, Annie and her older sister went north to work for affluent families. The two sisters sent money home to help their father buy land. Annie recalled her mistress's love of the game Parcheesi, and part of her job was to be her partner in the game. After marriage, Annie and George went to Pittsburgh where George found work. Upon returning to Powhatan, Virginia, with their first child, they made their home on James Morris's land in Mohemenco. My grandfather and father brought my mother, Clara, and me from St. Philip's Hospital in his black Ford.

Some of my earliest memories consist of leaving "the house on the road (Cartersville)" and going "down the house" to a fifty-four-acre tract of land with a pond, trees (oaks, pines, persimmons, walnut, etc.), fruit orchards, gardens (vegetable and flower), fields of grain, cattle, fowls and buildings (barn, chicken coops, mechanic workshop, outhouse, and hand-dug brick-walled well). In doors were a hand pump for water, a cooking stove with a warmer, woodstove and fireplace for heating. The main dietary items consisted of the following: fresh milk, churned butter, herrings, fresh fish from the James River, deer, rabbit, quail, squirrel, fried shad roe (spring), crackling (dried, fried meat skin-pork rind) bread, beef, pork, poultry, black molasses, fried salt pork, canned/fresh fruit and vegetable, soups/stews, homemade breads and desserts (cornbread, hoe cakes, biscuits, rolls, puddings (rice/tapioca/bread), sugar cookies, ice cream, fruit cobblers, pies (lemon meringue and sweet-potato [from Papa's prized crop]), cakes (pound and fruit), and fudge candy, etc. They were made from scratch, and no recipes were used. Adults partook of dandelion and white potato wine and persimmon beer. Grandfather would toss corn kernels on top of the stove to parch and then eat the kernels (not-popped corn).

Grandfather's front porch (with his handmade rails) was his favorite spot to relax in the summer. He could be found sitting on his toolbox at the west end of the porch in overalls and Brogan shoes opposite our favorite swing on the east side of the porch made by him. Grandmother would sit in a metal chair, barefooted, reading her Bible in the morning. Next she would prepare lunch. I disliked the days when rice was on the menu; she would put sugar on the rice, and I wanted salt. Grandmother attended Sunday school and church (our church Mount Zion held services once a month, second Sunday). Grandfather did not attend as often. She was the adult Sunday school teacher at Greenbrier and one of the first teachers at Mohemenco Community School, along with her sister Etta Taylor and Thaddeus Hewitt when it was organized. Later, graduates of normal schools replaced the parents. (After slavery, ex-slaves worked during the day and attended adult education classes at church using the Bible to learn to read.) Grandmother took us to Sunday school and required that we wear hats. This practice might have stimulated my interest in millinery at VCU's School of Fashion Design years later. Grandmother taught me how to draft patterns. In elementary school, I made skirts and blouses for myself and younger sister using printed flour sacks (plaid and beets designs).

My favorite time was Sunday's visit to my grandparents' home (except during the wintertime when the road was too muddy to drive, and we had to walk the one-half mile back to our "warm" home with a railroad lantern, fearing the sounds coming from the woods). We watched the television programs (*Lassie, Roy Rogers, Wild Kingdom, Ed Sullivan*, etc.). We sat in front of a roaring fire that warmed the living room. Grandfather (called *papa* by his children) smoked tobacco in pipes that he had made. They were displayed on the mantle over the fireplace along with a barometer. The aroma of the various tobaccos and the roaring fire created a magical environment. We snacked on homemade bread/meat and marbled cake. The best event occurred when Grandfather went to his wardrobe and returned with "goodies": graham crackers and peanut brittle. Stories of the past were discussed about his enslaved ancestors on Belmead. I listened.

During one of these discussions, Grandfather mentioned Philip St. George Cocke and the rumors about his death. Grandfather's stepmother (deceased by the war) and her two sisters were house servants. Oral history reports the following comment by the planter before he committed suicide in December 1861: "I cannot stand to see my daughters put their lily-white hands to toil." He also mentioned that his father, James Morris, told about a slave that created such havoc on the plantation that the owner had to intercede in his punishment—tying him to the rafters of a building and letting him remain for a time. He said Philip Cocke appeared to have been a fairly decent master to his slaves. Grandfather also mentioned "Black Sally," referring to the name blacks used for Sally Hemmings, and John Jasper, the renowned black preacher from Fluvanna, Virginia, who found Sixth Mount Zion Baptist Church (Richmond, Virginia) and was known for his sermon "De Sun do Move." He also mentioned that his brother had married a woman who was fathered by one of Philip's sons.

Ivory Emmett Morris

I questioned my father to find out more about Belmead's oral history and to find out what it was like to live in Mohemenco during his generation. Ivory Morris (1906–1999) was a master carpenter and carpentry instructor at St. Emma's Industrial and Agricultural Institute. White "professors" taught the academics, and the colored "instructors" were in charge of the industrial department. The founder stated that blacks were not allowed to rise above instructors. White professors lived on the "hill," and the black instructors lived at the "bottom of the hill" in a row of houses across from the creek. He also was a cabinetmaker, boat/ferry builder, gunsmith, game hunter, fisherman, and outdoorsman. He enjoyed walking through the woods and the land of Mohemenco with his children (four girls) and discussing the history of our homeland, as well as the fauna and flora. He commented, "Belmead property has secrets and unsolved mysteries. During an excavation project during the school's days, a pit of small bones was found. There were several instances where 'Belmead boys,' priests, and instructors fathered children with St. Emma Parochial students from Mohemenco, and there were cases where St. Francis de Sales girls were caught in the cadets' dormitories and dismissed from the school." He recalled the sad day when an African American employee was shot and killed by another African American employee in retaliation for constant teasing (1960s). The killer spent the rest of his life in prison in Powhatan.

My father shared with me details of life in Mohemenco Hamlet. He described how hogs were slaughtered in the cold weather and the meat stored in the smokehouse on rafters. Sometimes rats would get to the meat and leave only the skin. Next he talked about taking tobacco to the market in Richmond, a thirty-mile drive. The farmers used wagons and horses. They would heat bricks in the fireplace overnight and arise early in the morning and put these bricks on the wagon's floor to keep their feet warm, dress in heavy clothing, and wrap themselves in blankets. Lanterns were used to light the way. It was a four- to five-hour trip one way. They arrived by noon and sold their tobacco for cash. They reheated the bricks in the marketplace and ate their meal. One relative would burn a $20 bill in gratitude for his successful harvest. They started back to Mohemenco with the cash. To prevent highway robbers from taking advantage of them, they had a party of several "strongmen" drivers and armed men for protection. They arrived safely home at dust.

Next he told me about three practices that blacks encountered during travel. When taking the bus to and from Richmond, Virginia, to New York City, scammers would approach riders and tell them that they had found a wad of money and would share it with them if they would go on a back street near the bus station. Once on the street, riders were robbed and beaten. Another practice involved tying a wad of money to a string and placing the money in the middle of a well-traveled road. Those who stopped to pick up the money were attacked. Crossing the James River on the Maiden Bridge in Michaux could present problems at times. In the earlier days, the bridge had one lane for crossing. The accepted rule was to allow the vehicle that was on the bridge to cross the James River. However, a racial incident occurred when a car of African Americans was on the bridge. A white driver demanded that they back off the bridge and allow him to pass. The African American driver told the man to back off the bridge or be thrown into the river. The man became fearful and allowed the blacks, who had the right of way, to cross. The blacks, fearful of some sort of retaliation, sped to Richmond. The driver was Ivory's brother-in-law.

I questioned my father about his survival during the Depression era. He said that he did well. He had left Belmead for a period and was living in New York during the Depression. He held several jobs—elevator operator, porter, janitorial, etc. This information surprised me. I knew he was a carpenter and wondered why he did not work in the carpentry trade. Later, I realized that this trade was not open to African Americans nor membership in the trades union. He said that he witnessed the building of the Empire State Building. My parents were married in New York City in 1930.

They enjoyed living up north among their relatives and other people who had gone there to find economical opportunities that were not available in Powhatan, Virginia. My parents had accomplished their goal—saved money to build a home in Mohemenco. In 1939, they returned to their hometown. My father and my grandfather built our home. They never had a mortgage nor homeowner's insurance. My father figured if the home was destroyed by fire, he could build another house since he was a carpenter. It was a cost-cutting measure to limit his expenses. Their New York travel trunks contained garments, pictures, and New York current events scrapbooks of African American history. They were kept in the attic of our home. I enjoyed looking through those trunks, which summarized the experiences of my parents in the big city. Unfortunately, these trunks and many family memorabilia were destroyed in the fire of 1978. This fire was one of two unexpected events in the 1970s that challenged the family's quality of life. The home was partially burned to the ground. The fire was caused by dust on old electrical wiring. My father and his cousin Winfred Taylor (former woodworking instructor at Belmead/SEMA) rebuilt the house. Earlier, after St. Emma's closed, my father and Winfred started a repair and renovation business specializing in cabinetmaking. My father was involved in a lawsuit involving questionable practices by county officials resulting in double deeding of land. He had paid taxes on the property for forty years. The house and land under question were deeded back to him as a case of adverse possession. More information about the life of Ivory Morris can be found in Powhatan County Historical Society's Oral History Project—"Ivory Emmett Morris" (1906–1999).

I enjoyed listening to and talking with my grandmother, grandfather, and father about our roots. I wish that I could speak with them to find answers to questions that I have not found. However, I am thankful that I had the experience of intergenerational interaction, which has enriched my life.

Sandra Morris-Kemp reflects on the reality
of Drake House (built in 1822)

Mohemenco Historical Marker, "Mohemenco and
Drake House" Erected by the Michaux—St. James
Foundation and Sandra Kemp, local historian.

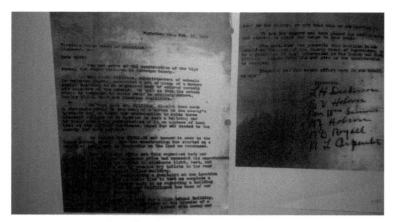

Reverend William Simms and others, 1937 letter
to Virginia State Board of Education
*Copy courtesy of The Sisters of the Blessed Sacrament

William Simms's and Bettie (Brown) Simms's
Wedding Certificate (1891). Original copy
found in Reverend Simms's Church Bible.

1927 Letter to Ruby (Mayo—Farris) Weaver
from a Mohemenco resident (unknown)
*Photograph courtesy of Albert Weaver

"Ruby, Albert, and Suwon"
*Photograph courtesy of Albert Weaver of California

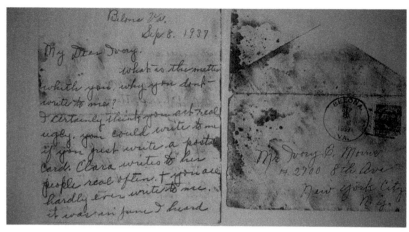

"Annie Morris's Letter to Ivory Morris in N.Y.C.
(1937). Envelope and page 1 of the letter."

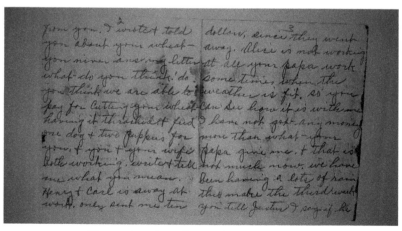

"Pages 2 and 3 of Annie's Letter (1937)"

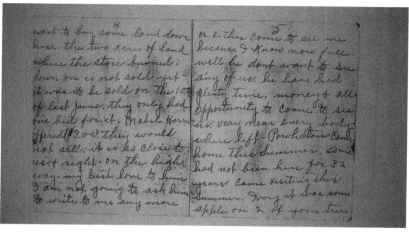

"Pages 4 and 5 of Annie's Letter (1937)"

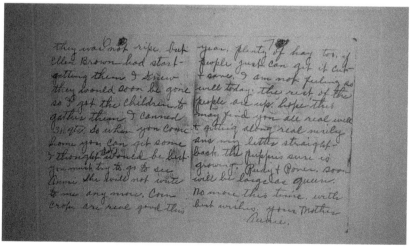

"Pages 6 and 7 of Annie's Letter (1937)"

CHAPTER 7

Experiences and Challenges in Pursuit of Higher Education and Career Advancement

Education

My first challenge, during the days of segregated education, came at the age of seven years (1952). It was a memorable year—chickenpox and my appearance in a play, *Ten Little Indians*.

After completing first grade with all Cs (commendable) and no Ss (satisfactory) or Us (unsatisfactory) on my report card, I was denied promotion to the second grade at Pocahontas Elementary Colored School by my teacher (her daughter was my fifth-grade teacher). My father consulted with the black supervisor of education/elementary school principal, who sided with the teacher to retain me in the first grade for another year. After receiving no reasonable explanation, my father contacted the Powhatan Public Schools Superintendent of Education. The white superintendent told my father and me that I would have to prove my ability. I was to be promoted to the second grade on a probationary status. I was required to show the results of testing for two weeks. I performed well on every test. By October, I was a full-fledged second grader. Later the principal commented, "The teacher enjoyed having the student and did not want to let her go." The second-grade class experienced two sad events: The loss of one of our classmates, who died in a fire one weekend. She was the only person that I knew who disliked ice cream! Another classmate's mother died. Our textbooks were discarded books from the white school. Our parents paid a rental fee for the use of these books.

In the third grade, I was allowed to "manage" the classroom in the teacher's absence. The teacher told me to write the names on the blackboard of any student who misbehaved. In the sixth and seventh grades, the teacher gave me permission to skip class time and serve as a cafeteria helper because of my advanced skills. In my days at the colored high school (eighth, ninth, and tenth grades), I excelled academically and, at semester sessions, received certificates of honor. If integration and changing schools had not taken place, I probably would have been the valedictorian of my class.

How many other systems have allowed teachers to continue in their positions when they were ineffective? I had assertive parents who valued education and would fight and make sacrifices for what was right. My role models were my grandparents, parents, and teachers who instilled values that provided the foundation for one to become a productive member of society.

My next challenge came during the integration era while attending Powhatan High School in the eleventh and twelfth grades (1963–1965). Powhatan had been the white high school and Pocahontas had been the black high school during the days of segregated education. In 1963, the courts ordered Powhatan County Public Schools Board to enroll sixty-five Africans American infants (legal term) to the former white elementary and high schools. I was one of these "infants." My sisters Maurice, Jewnita, and Alcibia were included. Our parents were Ivory and Clara (Carrington) Morris. I became the first African American graduate. A year earlier, the courts had ordered three preschoolers—Maria Morris, Pauline Evans, and Alcibia Morris—to enter the first grade and integrate the elementary school. The county officials stalled by manipulation of the pupil placement forms. The courts tiring of the tactics of Massive Resistance ordered integration of the elementary and high schools to include siblings of these three children and other children as long as the adult interested parties had legal guardianship of the child.

There were two other African Americans in the junior class, but they left in the senior year, leaving me to be the only black in the class. The teachers and students tolerated our presence. It was a very isolating experience; no one spoke to us or befriended us. One positive experience occurred when the chemistry teacher stated to the class that Sandra Morris had made the highest score on a chemistry test. I focused on my goals of making good grades and completing high school. In contrast, I remember negative experiences. My classmates' parents arranged a secret prom location, excluding the black juniors and seniors. When President John Kennedy was shot, some students applauded his death and made the following comment: "I wonder what the blacks are going to do now?" Stereotyped and racist statements were made. I overheard the comment, "Oh, I guess that is the NAACP Cadillac." No, the Cadillac belonged to my uncle, who was a successful businessman in Richmond. He allowed use of it to take me to graduation practice because my father's car was being repaired. The worst experience occurred when my senior homeroom/English teacher told me that I could not go on stage to participate in the baccalaureate and graduation activities because no one had ever missed the practices. She said it did not matter that I was sick. What a disappointment. I had purchased a white empire-style and a blue-and-white princess-cut lace dresses for these activities. My parents told my invited guests of the situation, and they walked out. A lawyer called Powhatan School System, and the matter was settled. I walked across the stage and received my diploma. My parents and other parents pushed for integration, not for a new black school building, new books, or to have their children sit next to whites. They wanted to end a dual school system that was supposedly separate and equal. In reality, the systems were unequal. They wanted subjects included in the coursework that would equip/prepare us for college entry and success without remediation or drop-out. They made sacrifices for us to have a better life, and they saw equality in education as the key.

Years later, one of my classmates told me at a class reunion that he wanted to tell me what a brave thing I had done. Another classmate who enrolled second semester of the senior year stated the following: "There were three cliques, the Nina of one, the Sandra of one, and the fifteen who stayed in the public schools." They did not attend the Huguenot Academy [private] started as part of Virginia's Massive Resistance movement to avoid integration of the public schools. The whites who stayed in the public schools had many reasons, but they were not about equality.

Years later, a history teacher, invited me to speak to several of his classes on my experiences as the first African American to graduate from the integrated school during Black History Month (2004). They invited me to their prom, and I attended. I also created a publication and presented a program to the elementary school assembly about the African American history in Powhatan, Virginia, during slavery, reconstruction, segregation, and integration. The *Powhatan Today* interviewed me on the fiftieth anniversary of integration in the county. I stood on the steps of my former high school, which is now a community building and safety/police offices. The nearby former elementary school is now the social services building.

Fifty years later, Pocahontas Middle School principal (African American) interviewed me and videotaped a session about my experiences being the sole African American in the twelfth grade during the integration of the school. At this time (winter 2014), the Pocahontas Middle School students were in the process of establishing a historic marker about Pocahontas High School. The marker erected in 2015 stands on Route 60 directly in front of my first-grade classroom where I was challenged by blacks to prove that I had mastered skills that would enable me to master second-grade work (1952). She asked me for advice to be given to the fifth and sixth graders. My reply was the following: develop core values of positivity, patience, and respect for others; become a productive member of society and self-actualized; make an effort to fight injustices and find a worthy cause to fight for; get a good education (to quote Herbert H. Humphrey, "It is so important to your own future and to your country"); venture outside of Powhatan and experience the world and prepare yourself for "global diversity"; and do not expect anyone to give you anything, work hard, and when people see that you are making an effort, they will help you, but you have to do it!

In the fall of 2016, a Pocahontas Middle School Revitalization Committee met to decide what to do with the school that had been

Pocahontas Elementary/High School in segregation days and the additions. The African Americans asked that the portion that was the original school be saved to become an African American history and education museum rather than demolish the whole complex. The adults who were first-grade students in 1951 told the committee how important it was to preserve this part of Powhatan's African American history.

In 1965 I left Mohemenco Hamlet and moved to the northern and western parts of the United States after graduating from Powhatan High School.

Before leaving Powhatan, I exercised my most basic right: I registered to vote. I voted at Mount Zion Baptist Church (founded by Reverend Alfred Morris, my great-grandfather's brother). My father stated, "You know who to vote for!" African American men had voted for Republicans since getting the right to vote shortly after the Civil War with passage of the Fifteenth amendment. The Democratic Party and the Byrd Machine kept African American voting Republican until the '60s. There was a Democratic candidate running (Kennedy) that African Americans knew very little about. Most voted for Nixon. I voted Republican like the majority of the blacks in Mohemenco. Later, the Democratic Party made inroads into the black population by running on issues of social justice and others. The party of Lincoln lost its appeal to most blacks.

Before graduating from Powhatan High School (June 1965), I applied to West Virginia State College, land grant university (now a University in Institute West Virginia, outside of Charleston) and was accepted into the college for the second semester in January 1966. Two individuals were instrumental in my acceptance: a reference from an alumnus of WVSC and daughter of William Washington. He was a successful farmer in Trenholm, Virginia, and businessman in DC. His home was designed by a Howard University architect. He was married to my mother's sister. The second individual was an admissions officer who gave "preferences" to rural applicants from Virginia.

During the Christmas holiday, I got a job in the kitchen of the tea room at Miller and Rhoads. (I had held part-time summer/

Christmas jobs in high school in the metropolitan Richmond area as a toy store clerk, CETA youth aide, and thread trimmer for Sears children dress line called Cinderella [a small county economic development project]). I spent the summers at home or visited relatives up north. When I was old enough to work, I found a summer job up north. The "experience" convinced me that such work was not what I wanted. The thought of the paychecks that would help with schooling expenses kept me from quitting.

On a cold and snowy day in January 1966, my parents took me to Mrs. Robert Bush's Rental Home where I had a room because the dormitories were filled (African American students from the north were the dorm residents, and white students were the day commuter students). This was the first time that I had experienced zero- and below-zero-degree temperatures. The smell from the nearby chemical plant with its continuous orange flame was sickening initially. In student orientation classes, I heard individuals such as Ruby Dee, Ossie Davis, and an action volunteer speak on social issues. (One student asked the volunteer if he had any political ambitions in West Virginia). The most enjoyable course was drawing. It was taught by a handicapped female instructor. One of my house roommates was an Iranian student, "Corkie." She was supervised by Dr. Olivia Kemp, who headed the foreign exchange program. Her brother Ira Kemp founded the Harlem (New York) Labor Union in the 1930s. Another brother, Maryland, was a munitions chemist at Fort Belvoir.

Another boarder was "Kay." She attended the Barbering College next to the college. Several of her siblings attended that same college. She went home to Rand, West Virginia, every weekend, and she invited me to go with her. I became part of Bob's and Rosa's family. A roadside historical marker in Malden tells the story of Booker T. Washington's beginnings in this mountain hamlet near Charleston, West Virginia, and the Kanawha River. Kay's and Sandra's meeting lead to a lifelong friendship over the miles. At age seventy-one, Kay operates her barbershop in Charleston, West Virginia.

While in West Virginia, I would visit my beloved relatives (Adams and Hamptons) who lived in the mountains and worked in the coal mines in the Tazewell-Bluefield area (a small place on the

West Virgina/Virginia line named Bishop). My relatives in Bishop, Virginia, call me "Sandyrose" or "Sandra Rose." I talked with Uncle Lem (Willie Hampton) about his experiences in the coal-mining industry. After retirement, he became a minister. He said that he was proud of the fact that he and others confronted management about black miners standing in water all day. Remedies were taken to end this practice. This town had a company store, and the whites lived on one street and blacks on another street in duplexes. Small boxes stood in front of each house to store the coal that was used for fuel. My daughter mistook them for doghouses.

Every summer, for as long as I can remember, my aunt and her family would visit us in Mohemenco. Due to segregation and lack of public accommodations for blacks, my aunt prepared food and drinks ("pops") for the trip. My father and uncle Lem fished the James River near Belmead during this weeklong vacation. Ivory and Lem played a joke on the game warden. They stayed on the river until 9:00 p.m., knowing that Lem had a fishing license. Mickey waited. When they debarked from the boat, Mickey asked Lem for his license. Lem handed it over. Dad and Uncle returned home with fish to clean and the details of the joke that they had played on the game warden.

In 1966, while returning from the spring semester at West Virginia State College late one night, we experienced the continued disregard for the recent laws passed concerning public accommodations. We stopped at a restaurant for takeouts. The management disregarded our presence. They questioned us about our ethnicity—"Are you all Indians?" Background comments included: "What are they trying to do?" I realized that the establishment had reservations about serving us. I explained that we were traveling from school back home to Virginia and only wanted takeouts. The hamburgers were prepared and given to us. On departing the establishment, I overheard the comment, "They must have some very high standards in Virginia." I did not understand exactly what was meant, but I had an idea. We ate the sandwiches, hoping that they were not "adulterated." We continued our journey!

I spent my summer in Jamaica Queens, Long Island, in the home of my aunt and uncle. My aunt had worked in Richmond as a childcare worker for a wealthy family, and my uncle had worked as a chauffeur. They both sought better opportunities and moved to New York. They met and were married in New York. They lived in a Brooklyn apartment. I spent a summer with them while I was in the elementary school. We did things that were fun and different from Virginia: Coney Island, Jones Beach, ate at an integrated lunch counter. They bought a home in Queens. My uncle became a union truck driver. I was shown the "Note" home of James Brown and told that a famous R&B singer lived in the neighborhood. My uncle drove from New York City to Connecticut, transporting merchandise for Bloomingdale's.

Through a contact of my uncle, I secured a summer job in the credit department at Bloomingdale's Department Store as a clerk. I noticed on the first day that I took the bus and subway to work, black specks appeared in my foundation. When I touched them, they smeared—pollution! One day, a famous singer came into the store, and a department was closed for several hours to allow her to shop.

New York was an exciting place, and I learned a lot about life. I heard new racial terms. I learned about theft rings who hijacked trucks of toys and other things. The souvenir that I received from my relatives (1950s) was a masked Zorro dressed in black on a black horse with a flying cape. The memento was lost when my parents' home was partially destroyed by a fire in 1978. I saw my first mega Kmart and visited a very large fish market on the bay. The concept of no salesclerks, only checkout clerks was new to me. The concept of eating fish for lunch or dinner was also new to me. My father relaxed in Virginia by fishing the James River and catching catfish, perches, etc. The next morning's meal was hot corn bread with butter and fried fish.

In 1966, I applied for admissions to Howard University, Washington, DC, and was accepted for September 1966.

Summer came and went, and I headed to DC. I arrived at Howard University and was assigned to Truth Hall. One of the residents on the hall was a drama student who later became successful in a television program. Another resident was the daughter of a well-known politician. My worst course was the required swimming. Stokely Carmichael appeared on campus, and radicals stood on the dining hall tables and gave speeches. It was a coincidence that seventeen years later at my grievance proceeding at Colorado State University in 1983 concerning equal pay, sexism, racism, and freedom of speech, the director of the women's program chose to read a social comment passage from Carmichael's book as the opening statement: "It is not the overt action that destroys, but it is the subtle covert action." I completed the year at Howard University.

During the summer of 1967, I went to New York City and stayed with my aunt and uncle. I found a summer temporary position working for a successful magic supplier. He needed zip codes added to the addresses of his customers to meet postal requirements. He said that if I took course work in accounting, he would hire me in his office. During the summer, my aunt and I went to baseball games. She knew that I admired Tommy Davis. One day, she took me to black Harlem, against her husband's wishes, for a tour and to visit a friend. One unfortunate event happened that summer: an "ethnic" shop relaxed my hair, and I developed scalp problems. In Richmond, a doctor who was the former employer of another aunt repaired the damage.

I had applied to *Virginia Commonwealth University's School of Arts* and had been accepted into the Arts Foundation Program. My goal was to pursue studies in fashion design and receive a BFA degree. In the fall of 1967, I entered the Arts Foundation program. I completed the first year arts foundation program. In art appreciation class, I was introduced to Jimi Hendrix as an art form. *Wow!* I was proud to see an American (African) artist with so much musical talent. In drawing class, I had to get over the shock of drawing nude live models. I applied to the fashion design program. I was accepted based on a worthy portfolio. The harassment and discriminatory acts that I endured for three years at the hands of the director of the Fashion Design Department were ridiculous and illegal.

I had struggled to get a National Defense Student Loan—equal opportunity for higher education without the financing to attend means nothing. Before receiving the loan, I had written a letter to Hubert Humphrey telling him of the problems that I and others were having in getting the loans. I was surprised to receive a response from him stating the following: "A good education is so important to your own future and to your country." He said he was referring my concerns to HEW officials. (The Minnesota Historical society has authenticated the signature as that of Hubert H. Humphrey.) I was not going to let anyone interfere with my goals.

Her discriminatory acts and most outstanding racial comments include the following:

1. A classmate and friend reported to me that the director had allegedly referred to me as "uppity."
2. Your work is not good, but I allow you to stay because you are the first African American to be accepted into the department.
3. You are attractive, and I cannot praise you too much because the white girls will get jealous.
4. Your buttocks are not flat enough.
5. I have helped you to steam your garment, and it has resulted in a steam burn on my arm—oh, I'll just have to wear long gloves tonight because my husband, a businessman, and I have been invited to an affair by the governor, and I don't want to appear as a "charwoman."
6. I don't like "Afro" hairdos. (I had changed my hair from a long page-boy style to a "bush.") Later she commented that since it was a curly style versus a kinky one, it was acceptable. (I wore the style as long as I desired, and my classmates were fascinated about the process involved.)
7. Do not illustrate models with African features and hairdos.
8. Do not add skin tone to the models; leave them "white."
9. Using primitive societies' clothing for inspiration is not preferred.
10. I did not want you to be featured on the video; I had someone else in mind. (This was the highlight of my ongoing "tussle" with the director. In an advertising videography clip for our upcoming fashion show, a local television channel chose me to preview an example of the garments.)

I could go on with the attempts to intimidate me. One gets the idea of what it was like to be an African American at this time in our history.

My father commented that my grades did not reflect my hard work and dedication. I persevered. By the end of the third year, the director commented, "Your work is really good [grades changed from Cs to As and Bs in the Fashion Department]." I had no problems in making good grades in the required retailing and art history classes. Art history appeared to be the most difficult course for a lot of the students. In those days, the classes were held on the top floor in the "Mosque" building (later renamed).

Back then, the program was racist and elitist. It was a woman's finishing school that was very class-conscious and cliquish. Very few worked in the field; most moved on to marriage. Many found work at the telephone company, department stores, etc. Wealthy students were allowed to pay another or fellow students to illustrate their designs or complete their designs. No criteria existed, only the director's subjectivity. "Working-class" students were typically terminated from the program with the comment, "You are just not skilled enough to stay in the program." It was not a true bell curve of learning.

I specialized in millinery (lost art) and took the required fashion design courses of sewing, tailoring, drafting, draping, illustration, and design. I still have my senior portfolio of twelve designs. My designs were inspired by primitive societies in North America and Central America (Navaho and Lacondone), Eastern Asia (white hairy Ainus), and Africa (Mangbettu and the Zulu of Southeast).

My family attended the Fashion Department's annual junior and senior fashion shows at Thalhimer's Store. They observed their sister/daughter and cousin Deborah (first African Americans models) walk down the runway with Afro hairdos and in garments designed by Sandra Morris. The theme was "Spain." My two garments were "Torrid" and "Gypsie." Two weeks later, they attended my graduation from VCU with a bachelor of fine arts degree. I was the first African American to graduate from the Department of Fashion Design in

May 1971. I had supportive parents who believed in me and challenged me to excel.

Finding a full-time, well-paying job in the field of fashion design was not possible for me. I made a compromise. I decided to pursue a vocational job in the field of education and pursue fashion as an avocation. The following are some of the attempts that I made to explore opportunities in the field of art and the responses:

1. Newspaper art department in DC: "Take more art courses."
2. Federal government printing/engraving apprenticeship program in DC: "No openings, lengthy program, very competitive."
3. Scarf design company in New York: "Your fabric illustration skills are very good. However, I will not hire you because the girls in the back will not be receptive to you. You should be in fashion. You have to know someone in this city to get in the industry (a referral was given)."
4. Fashion magazine in New York: "Your typing is excellent on your résumé [done by a résumé service], perhaps a job as a typist [low pay]."
5. Fashion designers in New York: "Unfortunately, we are downsizing. The design industry has moved overseas."

During the period of 1988 to 1995, I operated a correspondence program in hat making. I received a certificate to operate a proprietary school through the Commonwealth of Virginia Board of Education offering instruction in custom hat making/correspondence (*Hat Making Made Simple*, copyright and a trademark for "The Milliner"). I received technical assistance from the US Small Business Administration and Women's Network for Entrepreneurial Training Program. Many students enrolled in the self-tutorial program. The enrollees were from the United States, Caribbean, and foreign countries.

Years later (1998), I donated five of my creations (including patterns and illustrations) to the Valentine Museum's clothing collection: coat, jumpsuit, vest, suit, cocktail dress, and two-piece evening gown. In the Valentine's "Our Hearts on our Sleeves," third annual costume and textiles exhibition (April 28, 2017–January 28, 2018), two of my garments with illustrations were displayed: green organdy, beaded cocktail dress, and black silk two-piece embroidered evening dress. On April 26, 2017, I attended the reception to celebrate the opening of the exhibit. At the annual Rassawek Vineyard Spring Jubilee (Columbia, Virginia), held June 1–2, 2018, my millinery designs were displayed as well as items used to block and sew hats. (Also on display was a 1920 ferry that had been recently recovered from the bottom of the James River. The ferry builders were my father and grandfather.)

Employment

African Americans in Caribbean Peace Corps Volunteer Service, Woodward and Lothrop Management Training Program, Political Activities, Home Ownership in the Historical "Greenbelt Experiment" Renovated Community, and the University of Maryland School of Agriculture Higher Education Program as Students and Faculty

After graduating from VCU in 1971, I applied to the Peace Corps. (The first initiative for the Peace Corps came from Senator Hubert H. Humphrey, Jr. [Democrat, Minnesota]. He introduced the first bill to create the Peace Corps in 1957). I was accepted for Jamaica XII as a community development/crafts cooperatives officer. During the summer, I took my first plane flight across the country from Richmond, Virginia, to California. Our group did an urban live-in in San Diego, California. We lived with inner-city families and received training during the day at a local school. The staff prepared us for living in rural Jamaica. Long hours were spent in training. We relaxed on the beach of the Pacific Ocean in La Jolla, California. The calm water was quite a difference from the Atlantic Ocean in Tidewater, Virginias (150 miles from Mohemenco, Virginia). Other activities included visiting the California state fair and touring San Diego. We visited Tijuana, Mexico, to observe the rural and urban lifestyles. A task for the staff was to meld farmland youth and a few "rich" youth from the north with African Americans (mostly urban). Many whites had very little or no contact with African Americans. The urban live-ins helped. The interaction between the groups took time to develop and create a cohesive group ready to take on the work in Jamaica. Once the task was accomplished, we were finally ready to go to Jamaica!

We flew to Jamaica and settled in at a local college. The long hours of training resumed. Lecturer Rex Nettleford gave a most electrifying all-day presentation on the culture of Jamaica. We were taught how not to be an "ugly American." The concept of "Jamaican white" (racial category) differed from the American concept of white. Next we were assigned to hosts who would sponsor our live-ins, rural or urban. I ended up living with a working-class family in the country. Electricity was unpredictable. Rats disturbed my sleep at night. I threw items at them. The mongoose had gotten rid of the snakes on the island. With the snakes gone, the rats proliferated. At their home, I was introduced to a dish called ackee and salt fish. The seeds looked like eyeballs. I was told that they were poisonous when not ripened and gas-filled. A lot of cheese and mangos were served. Volunteers relaxed by visiting one another in the different locations, taking trips to Kingston or Montego Bay. The most unusual dish was having goat-meat (with chopped bones left in) soup. Some volunteers visited rum bars/night spots.

There was an underlying question with which the Peace Corps had to contend. Jamaica had always had white volunteers, and the present group included African Americans. Would the Jamaicans accept the five black volunteers? The potential problem never surfaced; we were accepted!

The poverty that I witnessed was unbelievable. I worked with the women in childcare, nutrition, sewing, and crafts development. I realized how blessed I was. I understood how poverty and lack of educational opportunities are limits to self-actualization and success in life. I had ventured outside of my "small world" and embraced another culture. I acknowledged diversity. This experience led to my commitment to continue to fight barriers to equality. I recall the friendship and support of my fellow African American volunteers. I returned to Jamaica a second time for a vacation. With three Jamaican agriculture workers/teachers and a volunteer, I traveled across the island and visited the Blue Mountains, a fortress, and Montego Bay. We dined on meat patties along the way. I experienced the majestic view of the Caribbean Sea the night before my departure. The next morning, I dined with my friend (Peace Corps volunteer) on a meal of eggs, meat, and sliced tomatoes (new to me) while looking at the docked ship *Hope* and the towering cement factories. Later, I boarded the plane and flew back to the metropolitan Washington, DC, area to my retailing job.

My retailing career started with a brief stay in sales at Saks Fifth Avenue in Chevy Chase, Maryland, while waiting for an opening in the Management Training Program at Woodward and Lothrop (Woodies) in Washington, DC. I applied for the program. The store accepted me into the program. In the '70s, African Americans were accepted into the program with no planned opportunities for advancement. I worked in the contingency squad (filling in for short areas). This gave me an opportunity to learn about retailing while waiting for an opening in the management field. A position was offered. I accepted the position as an assistant buyer of books. I was excited. It was short-lived. I spent my time loading books at the warehouse, not learning purchasing skills. The only excitement in that position was seeing a well-known designer of jeans arriving in a limousine (tanned, very thin, and dressed in brown) and entering the store for a book-signing event.

I went to Human Resources and asked for a transfer. I was assigned to the Chevy Chase location as an assistant department manager for blouses and neckwear. The excitement soon wore off. I found myself on the floor selling and unpacking boxes of merchandise. I quickly purchased "comfort" shoes to accommodate the long hours of standing. I had no stock/floor staff to supervise because of the absenteeism of the clerks. My managerial duties had to be neglected. I did enjoy the 20 percent discount that I received on store purchases.

The straw that broke the camel's back was an incident that occurred on inventory night when the assistant store manager reprimanded me for not having all my merchandise "tagged." She pointed out how the sportswear department manager in the adjacent space had all her merchandise in perfect order. This employee had dependable floor staff and stock persons. She was able to stay in her office performing her managerial duties. Basically I was given impossible tasks and expected to perform miracles. Overall, the management training program did not provide proper training that was needed to succeed. I resigned from my position and made plans for the future— seeking better working conditions (nine to five/forty-hour workweek and no holidays, weekends, or night work), financial security which would allow me to leave the home of my relatives and get an apartment near to work (the Washington House on Sixteenth Street), and finance my education.

My plans included finding new employment that offered career advancement opportunities and pursuing higher education credentials at night. I took brush-up courses in typing and shorthand (*ABC vs. Gregg*—the owner of the business school had developed this easy type of shorthand). During the period of 1973 to 1978, I worked as a stenographic secretary for the National Grange (a farming lobbying/ fraternal organization), the federal government, and taught job readiness skills at a proprietary school during the day and evening. I took teacher certification courses at Minor's Teacher College, Washington, DC. During that time, I met Darryl R. Kemp (son of Elmer and Louise [Allen] Kemp). We became engaged in 1973, and in 1976, we were married in a civil ceremony in Rockville, Maryland. We flew to NYC for a brief honeymoon.

In 1975, I applied to the *University of the District of Columbia* (land grant university), also known as Federal City College. I was accepted into the adult education program (study of sociology, psychology, and education). I specialized in gerontology (the scientific study of the phenomena of aging) and supervision. I received training in important principles—Malcolm Knowles's principles of andragogy, Abraham Maslow's hierarchy of needs, Peter Drucker's management by objectives, etc. I completed an internship in office

125

skills at Opportunities Industrialization Center (government employment training program) and adult special education at Kennedy Institute. My thesis was "Creative Use of Leisure Time: Roosevelt Hotel for Senior Citizens." My practicum involved teaching arts and crafts to seniors at several centers. At one activity, I met an Italian American ex-priest from Boston who was director of Senior Citizen Activities at the Republican National Committee. He spoke to the seniors about social ills and social justice. He liked my work with the seniors in the community and appointed me to the role of senior citizen leader for DC. It was exciting to work for senior citizen issues. After attending classes three nights a week for two years of study (4.0 grade point), I received my master of arts degree (1977).

In 1977, my husband and I bought a cooperative unit in Greenbelt Homes Inc., Greenbelt, Maryland. These homes had been built after the Depression. It was one of the projects of the New Deal. The community was predominately white. Minorities were encouraged to apply to accommodate the requirements of the massive renovation of the community by Housing and Urban Development. Greenbelt is close to College Park, Maryland, site of the University of Maryland (land grant university).

In 1978, I applied to the adult, continuing, and extension education (formerly rural education) program in the School of Agriculture at the University of Maryland (UM). At the same time, the School of Agriculture was attempting to expand or diversify their teaching faculty and increase the enrollment/employment of minorities in their higher education programs. I was accepted into the program. My graduate teaching assistant (GTA) assignment was to assist with the teaching of the course youth development. At the same time, I was to pursue a doctorate in youth development and program planning. Part of my responsibilities was to bring speakers from youth organizations to the class. I asked my former employer, director of Youth Activities at the National Grange, to speak at the orientation program. I had worked two years at the grange as a secretary. The National Grange is a farming lobbying/fraternal organization. It is the headquarters for the grandmaster and youth program at the national level and is located near the White House. President Dwight D. Eisenhower wanted farming input nearby.

It was quite a challenge to assist an assistant professor who was on the line; he had to "publish or perish." The GTA responsibilities interfered with my doctoral studies. Our advisor had to remind the department chairman that the eighteen minorities were there primarily to attain their degrees, thus allowing the School of Agriculture to increase its minority graduates and staff. A more balanced workload was enacted. My research focused on "Developing Strategies to Enhance Adult Motivation to Participate in Programs and Activities." The hardest course was statistics. The atmosphere in the department was acceptable. One bathroom's graffiti reflected racial prejudice: "The buffalo is proof that the African American and the Native American mated." I completed my doctoral coursework and designed the research study: self-learning vs. the dynamics of group learning. I did not carry out the experiment. I took a break from my studies at the University of Maryland.

Women in Nontraditional Careers—Trade Unions, Military, and Small-Business Entrepreneurship

In 1980, I applied for two apprenticeships in the trades. I passed the tests for the sheet metal and steamfitter trades. I selected the sheet metal trade. I worked in the field during the day and attended the schooling program at night. I found the handling of the fiberglass insulation unbearable. The schooling was easy. I had coursework in geometry. This training was very helpful. I saw a number of the men failing the program because they could not pass the coursework. The goal was to go from an apprentice to a journeyman. A remedial training program was established to remedy this part of the program in response to a lawsuit that had been filed to increase the number of women and minorities in the trades program. Since I came from an art background, I was promised an office position as a drafter. I decided to join the Army National Guard instead. I wanted a nontraditional training military occupation specialty (MOS). I passed the test and was accepted into the Utilities Equipment Repairer (UER) program. Basic training took place at Fort Dix, New Jersey. The most feared activity was going through the gas chamber. Some of the other challenging training activities were the night fire, obstacle course, driving a tank, campouts, timed mile run (even with Achilles tendonitis, I made it), and the grenade throwing. Who can forget KP, cleanup, inspections, pushups, and marching? Some enlistees initially believed they had made a mistake. We learned discipline and became physically fit. Enlistees graduated and went to MOS locations. I went to Fort Belvoir School of Engineering for UER training.

My training prepared me for a position as a mechanic for the U-Pack gas turbine generator that operated the Pershing missile and the portable hospital, MASH (mobile army surgical hospital). We marched with briefcases. There were two females in the class. The class members helped one another on the theory and hands-on training because we wanted members to make their goals—passing the course and going permanent party overseas or going to our reserve units.

A couple of the young men confided to me that prior to enlistment, they were drug dealers. They said that dealing drugs was the only employment opportunity in their town, but they realized that this activity would only lead to bad records, jail, prison, or death. They saw the military service as a way out—completing their education (GED) and career training. Opportunities should exist for youth to have access to job readiness skills, work experience, and mentoring for careers. The military is one career opportunity. Others include job corps, peace corps, trades, community college, and college/university.

I graduated and began my monthly reserve training at Fort Mead, Maryland. At one weekend training, several female medics were standing around the generator for the portable hospital. As an officer approached, one said to me, "We should leave." I proudly said, "I am a mechanic for the U-Pack generator, and I do not have to leave." I continued my studies at UM and attended my reserve meetings. Shortly after returning from the first training, the unit asked me to take advanced training in the field of biomedical repair in Colorado. In 1981, I accepted the offer and again took leave from UM and went to Fitzsimmons Army Medical Center in Denver, Colorado, for training. While I was vacationing in Florence, Colorado (site of the present supermax prison), I saw an advertisement for a home extension agent in Colorado. I liked Colorado. After completing my training, I applied for a position in the extension service. After several interviews, a position was offered to me. I accepted the full time position with Colorado State University (land grant university) as a 4-H extension agent/clothing and textiles resource specialist for the seven-county southeast area in the High Plains District. While working at CSU, I completed my remaining UM requirements and later received an advanced graduate specialist (AGS) certificate and went on inactive military reserve status.

Colorado State University/Colorado State Board of Agriculture
Equal Pay and Free Speech

I began my assignment in the summer of 1981 in the Kiowa County (Eads) extension office as a United States Department of Agriculture Cooperative Extension agent. I worked with the youth and homemaker clubs in Haswell, Towner, Eads, Sheridan Lake, Brandon, Arlington, and Chivington. I also worked with the youth and homemakers clubs in the counties of Baca (Springfield,) Bent (Las Animas), Cheyenne (Cheyenne Wells), Crowley (Ordway), Prowers (Lamar), and Otero (La Junta/Rocky Ford). The area office was in Lamar (Prowers County). I was the first African American to serve in this area. My coworker worked with 4-H/youth and livestock programs. We shared responsibilities for the Kiowa County Fair and the Colorado State Fair in Pueblo, Colorado. We had an office secretary. Professional development workshops were held at CSU (Fort Collins, Colorado) and district meetings in Colorado Springs. Our area newsletter, *Current Comments*, and the local newspaper, *Kiowa County Press*, contained information on 4-H and home economics events and educational tips.

Kiowa County is a small rural/farming community on the high plains in southeast Colorado near the western border of Kansas. It was founded in April 11, 1889, as a railroad town. The county was predominantly white. Other counties in the USDA Extension area included Hispanic populations. The settlers of Kiowa County had come from Kansas in covered wagons and immigrant trains from the north. The chief industries included growing wheat; raising cattle, hogs, and sheep; feed lots; bull testing; and oil production. Many farmers received government subsidies for not growing certain crops. Some residents received government check for documented Native American heritage. The United States Department of Agriculture loan officer was an African American. His office was in Lamar, Colorado. His wife was very active in 4-H activities and served as a leader for many years. Their two daughters were involved in 4-H activities. In the 1980s, Kiowa County was listed in a major publication as having no unemployment. There was a shortage of housing. We purchased a mobile home and placed it in a rental park.

Kiowa County is the area where the Sand Creek massacre occurred (November 29, 1864) when General Chivington and 657 soldiers attacked and killed Arapahoe and Cheyenne Native Americans, including old men, women, and children. In 1983, after returning from a twelve-hour youth exhibit day at Plainview High School, my car went off the road and came to rest in a plowed field opposite the Sand Creek site. The secretary called the incident "the revenge of the Native Americans." US ex-senator Ben "Nighthorse" Campbell (Democrat turned Republican), Native American, had a historical marker erected at the site in 2007. Two historical forts are in the area: Old Bent's Fort (Otero County) and Fort Lyon (Bent County). Bent's Fort was a settlement on the Santa Fe Trail, and Fort Lyons was the staging point for General Chivington.

Initially, things went well. I was accepted by the people of the community and coworkers. I enjoyed my work and the experience of "wide-opened space" (tree less and more cattle than people). However, I disliked the experiences of having large cattle and grain trucks behind me while driving across the area for workshops. I would pull over to the roadside, allowing the truck drivers to pass and me to continue my travel! There was one "secret" problem that female agents faced in some offices. Two record filing systems had to be maintained. Sometimes information placed in the office file mysteriously disappeared. I kept my records in the office file and in my desk file. One female agent kept all of her records in the trunk and back seat of her car. I heard a few off-color comments: an older man at coffee break during the Christmas holiday referred to Brazil nuts as "Negro toes" (this was not Western terminology; some Virginians also called the nut by that name); use of the word *savage* to describe one's tousled hair; and the ability of the "wet back" to use pebbles to accurately count sheep passing through a chute.

In 1983, I reviewed salary increases and performance evaluations for the office. I noticed that the male agent's increase was above the approved increase, and my increase was below the approved increase. The performance reflected the same pattern—higher performance evaluation for the male and lower evaluation for the female. I contacted the area director and the district director and asked for a meeting to discuss my questions. I did not receive a satisfactory explanation.

Shortly thereafter, I received a letter from a probationary female agent telling me what a "terrible clothing workshop" the clothing and textiles specialist (CSU-tenured professor) and I (clothing and textiles resource person for the Southeast Area) had presented at the district meeting. I sent the letter to the director, and she was fired immediately. Tired of these harassing and discriminatory activities, I filed a complaint through the university's Grievance Procedure for the Resolution of Complaints of Discrimination in 1984. An American Civil Liberties Union lawsuit was filed later.

The following summarizes the complaint: Historically male extension agents were given higher salaries than female agents. The United States Department of Agriculture Cooperative Extension Service continued the practice of awarding males higher salaries because they supposedly had to support a family, and female employees did not. Extension stopped the illegal practice when federal laws, regulations, and executive orders prohibiting discrimination in educational institutions and agencies were enacted. They included Executive Order 11246 as amended by 11375, Title VI of the Civil Rights Act of 1964, Title VII (Section 799A) and Title VIII (Section 845) of the Public Health Service Act, as amended by the Comprehensive Health Manpower Training Act and the Nurse Training Amendments Act of 1971, Title VII of the Civil Rights Act of 1964, as amended by the Equal Employment Opportunity Act of 1972, The Equal Pay Act of 1963, and Title IX of the 1972 Educational Amendments. To substitute for the loss of higher salaries for males, the service initiated a practice of giving male agents higher salary increases with higher performance evaluations to justify the higher increases. In the long run, this practice resulted in lower salaries and less retirement benefits for female agents. For example, in 1984, the Board of Agriculture approved a 6.2 percent salary increase. The complainant received a 4.5 percent increase, and her coworker received a 7.6 percent increase plus a $300 merit increase and a higher performance evaluation. A discrimination complaint was filed through the grievance complaint procedure based on the following: an increase less than an across-the-board increment approved by the State Board of Agriculture and a lower evaluation than deserved on the annual review. The hearing panel uncovered a pattern of discrimination based on sex. The director of extension was ordered to eliminate the discriminatory practice.

The case was voided because contact was made with the complainant's US senator during a formal hearing vs. an informal hearing. This was an alleged violation of the proceedings. Actually, the decision had been made before the letter reached the senator's office. Nothing in the grievance procedure forbade contacting an outside official during a formal or informal hearing.

The American Civil Liberties Union (ACLU) petitioned the US Supreme Court to review the decision of the Colorado Supreme Court on the issues of the right to petition and speak on a matter of public concern. The United States Supreme Court denied the petition in 1990. Twenty-nine years later (2019), President Trump signed an executive order requiring US colleges to protect free speech on their campuses or risk losing federal research funding (by the Associate Press, *Richmond Times Dispatch*, Friday, March 22, 2019).

In 1985, I resigned from the Colorado State University/US Cooperative Extension Service and relocated to the Mile High City, Denver, Colorado. We purchased a townhouse in the metropolitan

Denver area. I worked part-time for the Denver Public Schools adult education program. In the evenings, I taught clothing/textiles skills to senior citizens at Denver Public Housing units and other senior centers. The goal was to encourage seniors to use their leisure time creatively. While teaching millinery in adult education classes, I wrote a millinery book and curriculum guide; drafted patterns, illustrated cutting and construction steps for sewing fabric hats and blocking straw and felt hats; produced a video; and made a sample line of hats in preparation to apply for a license to operate a correspondence program. The course was Hat Making Made Simple.

In 1988, my family left Colorado and moved to the metropolitan Richmond area and purchased a home in Henrico County. I applied for a position with the Powhatan County Public Schools. My educational level, post graduate, did not qualify me for a substitute position. Several white students of the 1960s were hired by the county as teachers. Shortly after returning to Virginia, a "teachable moment" occurred. While we were crossing the street near the Virginia Commonwealth University campus, a carload of white youth screamed a racist comment. I ignored them. My five-year-old daughter asked me what that word meant. I took the opportunity to explain to her about unacceptable words and phrases that lead to negative concepts, low self-esteem, and stereotyping, etc. In addition to discussing racial name-calling, we discussed the "good hair" concept—a phrase used by some African Americans and one of my pet peeves. I explained to her that any hair that is clean and free of disease is good hair. It does not matter if the hair is long, short, straight, curly, or kinky. My daughter entered kindergarten with a culturally diverse group in Henrico County Public Schools.

I continued with the curriculum development of my hat-making course. I taught the course in adult education classes. Finally in 1992, the Commonwealth of Virginia Board of Education issued a proprietary school certificate to operate a hat-making program. From 1989 to 1997, I worked in the fields of gerontology, GED, and family literacy. I operated the millinery program in Virginia from 1992 to 1995. I made a decision to seek a full-time permanent position with the Virginia State government. I applied for a position as an instructor with the Department of Correctional Education.

Virginia Correctional Center for Women and Disability Discrimination

I was hired as an academic teacher (ABE/GED/LIP) with the Department of Correctional Education (DCE), Virginia Correctional Center for Women (VCCW) in 1997 and received a postgraduate professional license to teach in adult education. I taught inmates literacy skills, GED preparation classes, and consumer skills. A number of inmates served as my tutoring assistants. The students were dedicated and spent their time wisely. I enjoyed my work. It was rewarding to observe individuals reach their goals of passing the GED test and receiving certificates of completion at graduation exercises. I had dedicated coworkers. I received acceptable evaluations. In 1998, the state changed the policy on employee meals and personal items entering the perimeter. The stated goals were the following: reduce the amount of incoming items and time taken to search individual food products, reduce the chances of personal possessions becoming lost or falling into the hands of inmates, and to provide employees with the benefit of receiving a free meal during their work hours for those who desired to receive a meal from the dining hall menu.

This policy change presented a problem for me as a diabetic person. From the beginning of my employment, I carried my own lunch and ate at my desk and kept "sugar" items on my person to prevent low blood sugar episodes. I kept my diabetic testing supplies in my tote. The food provided was not appropriate for a diabetic person, and my diabetes was not being controlled. I complained, and an alleged "diabetic lunch/emergency snack" was to be prepared in the prison kitchen for me. This alleged accommodation did not work. I knew what food items were best for me to control my meal and emergency episode sugar levels. I also knew that diabetes is a chronic disease that must be controlled by diet, medication, and exercise; and if these guidelines are not followed, complications could develop with the eyes, kidney, heart, and limbs, etc. I was determined not to let anyone, including this African American warden, improperly manage my diabetes and cause complications that would affect the quality of my life.

The warden refused to comply with the Americans with Disabilities Act. She would not make reasonable accommodations in the workplace regarding my diabetic condition and allow me to manage my disease appropriately. Several measures had to be taken to resolve the issue. My physician wrote her four letters about the condition and accommodations. The requests were denied. Finally, the doctor discussed the possibility of a job transfer. Next, an attorney wrote a letter to the superintendent of schools, Department of Correctional Education, stating that the whole problem could be easily resolved by allowing me to have the reasonable accommodations that I sought or by transferring me to another acceptable school where there was no comparable objectionable policy standing as a hindrance to my legitimate health needs and rights under the Americans with Disabilities Act of 1990 (ADA). Dissatisfied with the warden's response, I filed a complaint with the Disability Rights Section, Civil Rights Division, United States Department of Justice alleging that the Virginia Department of Corrections violated the Americans with Disabilities Act of 1990. An investigator was assigned to the complaint in 1999.

The Disability Rights Section proposed a means to resolve the complaint through informal means. The investigator determined that my complaint was an appropriate candidate for referral to the Department of Justice mediation program designed to allow parties to resolve their ADA disputes quickly and satisfactorily. The respondent was forbidden from retaliation against the individual filing the complaint. In addition, the Department of Justice suspended any action pending resolution of the mediation. Participation in mediation allowed the respondent to complete the matter without the involvement of the federal government. An agreement was approved for mediation by both parties.

A settlement agreement was reached in *Sandra Kemp vs. Virginia Correctional Center for Women*. The Americans with Disabilities Act dispute was resolved through mediation on December 22, 1999. A letter from the investigator, Disability Rights Section, to the warden stated the following:

> Please be advised that the Department of Justice is closing this complaint under the ADA. Our investigation did not resolve whether any ADA violations took place. In light of other litigation priorities, however, the investment of further enforcement effort is not warranted at this time. Be aware that the complainant may be entitled to file a civil action under the ADA in United States district court. Additionally, any failure to comply with the ADA almost 10 years after its passage exposes you to future complaints and lawsuits. The Department can reopen this investigation upon receipt of such a complaint. We therefore urge you to review you legal obligations and institute program modifications, as appropriate, in order to avoid the imposition of monetary liability.

Because of health issues, I was placed on short-term/long-term disability. I retired from the position in 2011.

Retirement

Upon leaving the world of work behind, I began to pursue my avocational interests of researching and writing. My goal is to continue the project of preserving the African American history, heritage, and culture in the Mohemenco-Belmead area, Macon District of Powhatan County, Virginia. I hope that this publication will educate individuals about the African American experience in America from the perspective of one family's documented sojourn for equality during the periods of slavery, reconstruction, segregation, and integration.

Six significant projects in historical preservation include the following:

1. Erecting a historical marker on my property on Bell Road (Route 684/ formerly Cartersville Road), "Mohemenco and Drake House" using my research findings
2. Having Drake House (also referred to as Falcon House) situated at the back of my property on Powhatan Lakes Road, documented as being built in 1822, using dendrochronology dating
3. Having matriclan testing done, which linked my ancestry with the peoples of Cameroon, Western Africa (Tikar, Bamileke, and Hausa)
4. Connecting and dialoguing between the enslaver and enslaved descendants from the Drake Plantation ("Coming to the Table")
5. Providing background information on the ferry recovered from the James River and displayed at Rassawek Spring Festival
6. Demonstrating the "Lost Art of Millinery" at Rassawek Spring Festival

My continuing education includes the following certificates: Leadership for Innovation and Change (1990) summer institute, NOVA University—Fort Lauderdale; Foundations for BeFriender Ministry-Minister/Trainer (2004), School of Divinity, University of St. Thomas; Pastoral Care and Counseling (2004), Richmond Hill; and Powhatan County Leadership Institute (2008), County of Powhatan.

Service on boards and committees include Francis/Emma Inc. (BELMEAD) Advisory Council, Board of Directors, Historical and Cultural Committee, co-facilitator of the Belmead Granary Planning Circle; Powhatan County Social Services Board; Tourism Board; Sesquicentennial Anniversary of the Civil War County Committee; War Memorial Building Use Committee; Chamber of Commerce Pictorial History Committee; and Pocahontas Middle School Revitalization Use Committee.

Bettie (Brown) Simms (1872-1965) "adopted" grandmother and father's cousin. Befriender to the Community of Mohemenco.

Grandmother Mary (Hazel) Carrington Farrar Black (1879-1967)
2014 Carrington Family Reunion quilt,
designed by Sandra Morris Kemp
Descendants of Mary (Hazel) Carrington Farrar Black

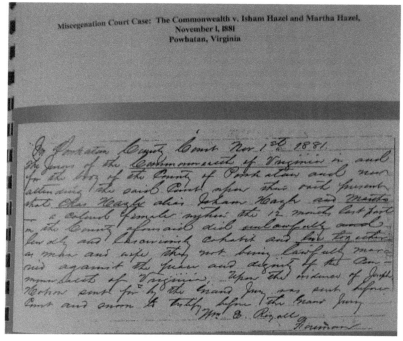

1881 Commonwealth of Virginia vs. Charles and Martha
Hazel (one of seven court appearances for violating
miscegenation laws forbidding interracial marriages)

"Sisters" Sandra (Morris) Kemp, Maurice (Morris) Hicks, Jewnita
(Morris) Tyler, And Alcibia Morris. Child: James "Jim" Hicks

Sandra Kemp's great grandparents, grandparents, and parents
Tyler Bell (1856-1943) and Ellen Bell (1856-1931)
George Morris (1874-1962) and Annie Morris (1879-1970)
Ivory Morris (1906-1999) and Clara Morris (1911-2000)

Ira Kemp, Founder of the Harlem (N.Y) Labor Union,
"Don't buy where you can't work," politician during the
1930s, and member of the Harlem Hellfighters (military)
Original copy found in estate papers of Bessie G. Kemp,
Washington, DC Afro American Newspaper employee

CHAPTER 8

Hope and Reparation

According to *Wikipedia*, reparation for slavery is the idea that some form of compensatory payment needs to be made to the descendants of Africans who had been enslaved as part of the Atlantic slave trade. Within the political sphere, only one major bill demanding slavery reparations has been proposed. This is the *HR-Commission to Study Reparation Proposals for African Americans Act*, which Representative John Conyers Jr. (Democrat of Michigan) has proposed to the United States Congress every year since 1989, though it has yet to be passed.[37] It is time for a dialogue and action on the issue of reparation.

Africans from Angola, West Africa, came to the Virginia Colony involuntarily in 1619. In 2019, the anniversary of the first four hundred years of people of African descent in English North America has been acknowledged.

In 1619, planter John Rolfe, widowed husband of Pocahontas, personally saw the arrival of Negroes near Jamestown from a Dutch or Portuguese man-of-war (the *White Lion*) and wrote:

> About the latter end of August, a Dutch man of war of the burden of 160 tons arrived at Point Comfort, the Comdor's name was Capt Jope, his

---

[37.] Cong. John Conyers, "My Reparation Bill—HR 40," Institute of the Black World, http://ibw21.org/commentary/myreparation-bill-40.

pilot for the West Indies one Mr. Marmaduke an Englishman. They mett with the "Treasurer" in the West Indies and determined to hold concort shipp hetherward, but in their passage lost one the other. He brought not anything but 20 and odd Negroes, which the Governor and Cape Merchant bought for victualle (where he was in greate need as he pretended) at the best and easiest rate they could. He hadd a lardge and ample Comyssion from his Excellency to range and to take purchase in the West Indies.[38]

Two hundred and twenty-two years later, my cousin Leander Sturdivant and other slaves owned by Sally Cocke Faulcon of Surry County, Virginia, rejected slavery in America and elected emigration to Africa as stipulated in her will for freedom or slavery. On June 1842, he and others boarded the *Miraposa*, which took them to Liberia, West Africa. Leander found work on a man-of-war.

On July 10, 1860, J. P. Skipwith (one of John Hartwell Cocke II's freed slaves) wrote the following from Africa:

Mrs. Faulcon's People is heaiar & doing well as can Expect. Leander the old man I have not seen him as yet He is on Board of the man of war His 3 Children Is hear in Monrovia. The 2 girls is maread. The boy is working at the Carpners trade.[39]

[38.] Bill Potter, "Africans Arrive at Jamestown," August 20, 1619, accessed August 21, 2017, http://landmarkevents.org/africans-arrive-at-jamestown-1619.
Public Law 115-102-January 8, 2018, http://www.gpo.gov/fdsys/pkg/plaw-115publ102.
H.R. 1242: 400 years of African-American History Commission Act, https://projects.propublica.org/represent/bills/115/hr1242
Deneen L. Brown, "Virginia to Mark 400 Years Since Arrival of Enslaved Africans," *The Washington Post*, Sunday, August 26, 2018, A14.
[39.] Randall M. Miller, ed., *Dear Master: Letters of a Slave Family*.

The American Colonization Society's and other repatriation groups' goals of resettling freed slaves, ex-slaves, and their descendants in Africa were not very successful. Blacks preferred to stay in the United States. They did not want repatriation—they knew nothing of Africa.

African Americans deserve recognition and economic redress for our contribution to this country. Our ancestors provided slave labor. The descendants of these slaves are struggling for social justice and equality. Reparation bills need to be enacted. This country should acknowledge that Reparation is overdue and take action to make it a reality.

Reparation should include more than some form of compensatory payment to the descendants of American who had been enslaved as part of the Atlantic slave trade. It should include help and payment for damages, losses, and suffering experienced by the African American descendants of those enslaved during the first four hundred years in the Colonies and the United States (1619–2019). The following cases of economic losses can be documented:

1. James Morris (1820–1902), Alfred Morris (1816–1882), and Melvina Jones (1835–1894). They were siblings and were born in Surry County, Virginia. They were chattel property of the Browne-Bowdoin-Cocke-Faulcon families on the Swann Point, Mount Pleasant, Four-Mile Tree (named for its distance from Jamestown) plantations in Surry County, Virginia; Belmead/Beldale plantations in Powhatan, Virginia; and the three Bremo plantations in Fluvanna, Virginia. My great-grandfather James Morris labored as a carpenter and miller (forty-five years enslaved), Alfred was a stonemason (forty-nine years enslaved), and Melvina was a field hand (thirty years enslaved). This slave labor is documented on the Negro 1854 and 1860 inventories from the Belmead Plantation (2,500 acres tract) in Powhatan, Virginia. After slavery, James worked as a sharecropper/miller during Reconstruction and post-Reconstruction on Belmead Farm and St. Emma's Agricultural

and Industrial Institute for Native American and Colored Youth before purchasing his first parcel of land in 1877 half a mile from Belmead. James Morris worked sixty-seven years in agriculture on Belmead property as a slave and ex-slave/freedman. Alfred became a Minister of the Gospel and became the first pastor/founder of First Antioch, Little Zion, and Mount Zion Baptist Churches in Powhatan, Virginia. He also served as a circuit minister for churches such as Hollywood Baptist Church in Powhatan, Virginia. Melvina married the ex-slave Charleston Taylor (carpenter). James, Alfred, and Charleston settled in neighboring Mohemenco Hamlet. During Reconstruction (1865–1877), they appeared on the 1870 census living as neighbors.

2. Sandra Rose (Morris) Kemp (born 1946) lost earning potential and retirement benefits and her job as a United States Department of Agriculture Cooperative extension agent due to the violation of the Equal Pay Act at Colorado State University (Land Grant University) as documented in the case of *Kemp v. Colorado State University and Colorado Board of Agriculture* (1984) in a questionable grievance procedure complaint hearing and a free-speech issue court case (1990).

3. Charles Isham Hazel (1835–1914), my maternal great-grandfather (white Confederate Civil War soldier from Spotsylvania County, Virginia), violated the Virginia Miscegenation Laws and married an African American woman (Martha Wood) shortly after the war. He appeared in Powhatan County, Virginia, court eight times (1879–1882) as documented in the case of *The Commonwealth v. Isham Charles Hazel*. In the early 1900s, he received a veteran's pension for a service connected injury/disability. One hundred and thirty-two years later in the same courthouse, his descendants lost three parcels of land in Powhatan County, Virginia, that Hazel had purchased in

the post-Reconstruction era in a questionable adverse possession court case (2013).

Our family has been denied justice and equality. Issues such as slave labor (unpaid), denial of equal pay, and land loss are three examples that should be addressed in a *United States Department of Agriculture Black Reparation Settlement Fund* (BRSF) for those who can document these economic losses.

African American ancestors were unwillingly taken from their homeland, forced to live in another part of the world, forced into enslavement, and regulated by codes that dehumanized them. African Americans have contributed greatly to the building of this country. The United States profited from slave labor. Payment for our labor has been delayed; it is overdue and should be paid. The acts of enslavement left the African American *scarred*. They have struggled to survive and recover from such treatment. Now is time for social justice and reparation to repair these damages.

African Americans continue to struggle for equality. They strive for a "decent quality of life" and the opportunity to achieve the "American dream" of having a decent paying job, purchasing a home, educating their children, having decent health care, etc. African Americans are plagued by many social problems that impact upon their existence. The descendants of slaves and ex-slaves face the issues of social ills.

According to Syracuse University, a "social ill," "social problem," or "social issue" exists when a condition is undesirable to some member of a community. Examples are crime, bullying, racism, delinquency, discrimination, family disintegration, drug addiction, and homelessness.[40]

Other social problems include violence/murder, police brutality/lack of safety, black-on-black crime, drug wars, hate crimes, gangs, missing/exploited/abused children, abuse of the elderly, partner/spouse abuse, massive incarceration, mental illness, substance

---

[40.] https://www.reference.com/world-view/definitions-social-ill-8e913e370e400 448.8/3/17.

abuse, illegal use of weapons/firearms, poor nutrition, lack of health care/untreated diseases (diabetes and hypertension), excessive use of tobacco and alcohol, joblessness/unemployment/underemployment (due in part to the closing of factories and jobs being transferred overseas), substandard and inadequate housing, poor education programs and dilapidated schools, lack of parenting skills, early childhood education deficiencies, teen pregnancy, single parenting, negative role models, negative use of leisure time, lack of youth development programs that include job readiness and work experience skills and career choice mentoring programs, etc.

Some form of redress, remediation, and reparation to African Americans should be considered for the things that have been taken from them. Program planning strategies should be developed to address the social ills (past and present) that are impacting negatively on their existence. Programs should be developed and implemented to provide solutions to these ills and give African Americans *hope* for a brighter future.

REPLY BRIEF FOR CROSS-APPELLANTS AND
APPELLEES

In The

UNITED STATES COURT OF APPEALS

For The Fourth Circuit

No. 8944.

EDWIN ALVIN BELL, et al., infants, etc.
Cross-Appellants and Appellees,

v.

SCHOOL BOARD OF POWHATAN COUNTY,
VIRGINIA, et al.,
Appellants and Cross-Appellees.

S. W. TUCKER
HENRY L. MARSH, III
214 East Clay Street
Richmond 19, Virginia

*Attorneys for Cross-Appellants and
Appellees*

The Press of Lawyers Printing Company, Incorporated, Richmond 7, Virginia

Bell et al v. Powhatan County School Board, Powhatan, VA.
Court case that integrated public school education in 1963.

THE VICE PRESIDENT
WASHINGTON

January 25, 1968

Dear Miss Morris:

Thank you for your letter telling me of the difficulty you have encountered in applying for a student loan.

I referred your letter to the U. S. Office of Education for their advice, and enclosed is a copy of their reply.

I know your experience has been discouraging, but I urge you to keep trying. It is so important to your own future and to your country that you get a good education. Good luck!

Sincerely,

Hubert H. Humphrey

Miss Sandra Morris
320 East Leigh Street
Richmond, Virginia 23219

1968 Letter from Vice President Hubert H. Humphrey to Sandra Morris concerning the issue of student loans and higher education ("Great Society" era)

Virginia Commonwealth University (VCU), School
of Arts, Department of Fashion Design. Deborah
Bell and Sandra Morris modeling creations by Sandra
Morris, 1971 at Thalhimer's Department Store.

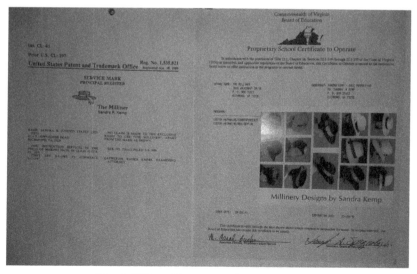

The Milliner Correspondence program:
"Hatmaking Made Simple" License, Trademark,
Millinery Designs by Sandra Kemp.

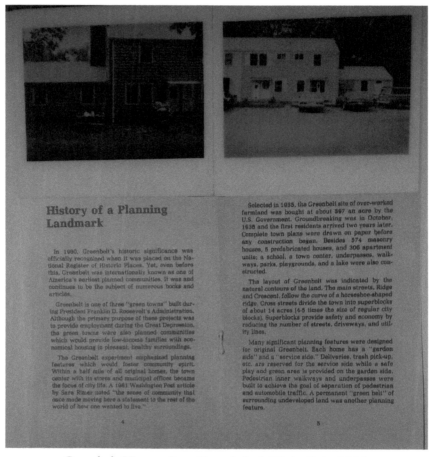

Greenbelt Homes, Inc. Greenbelt, MD, built in 1935.
A "New Deal" experiment in planned community living. Kemps
purchased a unit in the 1970s on Ridge Road. Left: Front Yard
Right: Parking/backyard

Sandra Kemp's Diploma (1981) from the U.S.
Army Engineer School, Fort Belvoir, VA

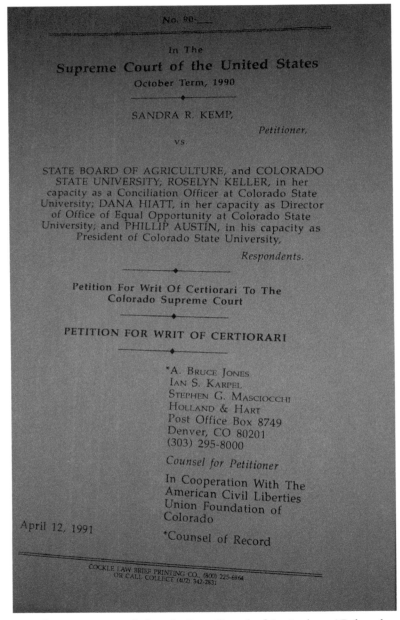

No. 90-___

In The

Supreme Court of the United States

October Term, 1990

SANDRA R. KEMP,

Petitioner,

vs.

STATE BOARD OF AGRICULTURE, and COLORADO
STATE UNIVERSITY; ROSELYN KELLER, in her
capacity as a Conciliation Officer at Colorado State
University; DANA HIATT, in her capacity as Director
of Office of Equal Opportunity at Colorado State
University; and PHILLIP AUSTIN, in his capacity as
President of Colorado State University,

Respondents.

Petition For Writ Of Certiorari To The
Colorado Supreme Court

PETITION FOR WRIT OF CERTIORARI

*A. Bruce Jones
Ian S. Karpel
Stephen G. Masciocchi
Holland & Hart
Post Office Box 8749
Denver, CO 80201
(303) 295-8000

Counsel for Petitioner

In Cooperation With The
American Civil Liberties
Union Foundation of
Colorado

April 12, 1991

*Counsel of Record

COCKLE LAW BRIEF PRINTING CO., (800) 225-6964
OR CALL COLLECT (402) 342-2831

Sandra R. Kemp v. Colorado State Board of Agriculture/Colorado
State University—Equal pay and Free Speech (1985-1990)

Philip A. Guarino's Reference for Sandra Kemp to
Colorado State University/Cooperative Extension
Service (United State Department of Agriculture)

AUG 2 1982

SANDRA R. KEMP IS THE NEW CSU Extension Agent for Eads. She reported for duty in Eads on Thurs., Aug. 19.

New Extension Agent Assumes Duties Here

Mrs. Sandra R. Kemp, who officially assumed her duties on Mon., Aug. 16, has been named the new Kiowa County Extension Agent with offices in the Eads Courthouse. She will be working with George Ellicott and her basic duties will be with the home and youth in Kiowa County. Mrs. Kemp replaces Mary Miller who transferred from the Eads office last year.

Sandra, who was born in Richmond, Va. and claims Greenbet, Md. as her home where she grew up, recently lived in Aurora just prior to moving to Eads. She and her husband, Darryl, who was recently on active duty with the U.S. Army Reserve, are slowly but surely getting settled down in Eads.

Mrs. Kemp attended the Virginia Commonwealth University where she received her Bachelor of Fine Arts Degree in 1971. She later attended the University of the District of Columbia where she received her Master of Arts Degree in 1977.

In 1978 Sandra enrolled at the University of Maryland where she did course work in Adult, Continuing and Extension Education. While attending the University of Maryland for three years, from 1978-81, she also served as a Graduate Teaching Assistant.

In addition to her formal education, Mrs. Kemp has held several positions which have rounded out her practical education. From June to Sept. 1971 she served as a member of the Peace Corps as a Home Economist and a Community Officer Trainee in Washington, D.C. After she left the Peace Corps she was employed by Woodward & Lathrop as a Management Trainee. After spending over a year with that firm she worked for four years as a secretary at the National Grange Headquarters and the Treasury, Bureau of Engraving and Printing in Washington, D.C. From there she entered the University of Maryland to continue her studies and to work as a Teaching Assistant.

Sandra said her hobbies include reading, writing, traveling, listening to good music and sewing. When asked what she thought of our big city of Eads she said she really liked it. She said she came from a small town, maybe just a little smaller than Eads, and was happy to get back into a small rural community.

She said that after her husband finds employment, and they get settled down, they plan to get involved in the community and get acquainted with the people.

Mr. and Mrs. Kemp · We welcome you to our community and hope we will make you "feel at home!"

"New Extension Agent Assumes Duties Here,"
photograph by Paul Daniels/Kiowa County Press
Credit: www.kiowacountypress.net

BIBLIOGRAPHY

Manuscript Sources

Private

"Cocke and Elliot Family Papers." Charlottesville, Virginia: Accession # 2433-ad, 2433 ae, Albert and Shirley Small Special Collections Library, University of Virginia.

"Holy Ghost Fathers." Pittsburgh, Pennsylvania: Duquesne University.

James River District Baptist Association. Richmond, Virginia.

"Sisters of the Blessed Sacrament." Ben Salem, Pennsylvania.

Virginia Genealogical Society. Richmond, Virginia.

Virginia Department of Historical Resources. Richmond, Virginia.

"Philip St. George Cocke Papers." 1854-1871, Mss1 C6455a. Richmond, Virginia: Virginia Museum of History and Culture, Virginia Historical Society.

Virginia Baptist Historical Society. Richmond, Virginia.

Public

"400 Years of African-American Commission Act." Public Law 115-102. January 8, 2018.

The Commonwealth of Virginia v. Isham Hazel and Martha Hazel. Powhatan, Virginia.

Edward Alvin Bell et al. Infants v. School Board of Powhatan County, Virginia and J.S. Caldwell. United States Court of Appeals, Fourth Circuit.

H.R. 1242: 400 Years of African American History Commission Act.

Library of Virginia: US Federal Census, 1850 and 1860 Slave Schedules; James Drake 1805 Plat, Powhatan, Virginia; Surry County, Virginia Will Abstracts; Surry County, Virginia Order Book (1838–1843, 187–188); Virginia Register of Deaths, Melvina Taylor (1894); Surry County, Virginia Will Book 1, p. 471, and 8 (1840-1845, 109–111, 435–436; US Federal Census 1870 and 1880; US Federal Special Census, Agriculture 1880.

"Reports of Deaths on Belmead Plantation." Powhatan County, Virginia, Clerk's Office, 1853–1865.

Sandra R. Kemp v. Colorado State Board of Agriculture and Colorado State University. Colorado Court of Appeals. Div. II.

Sandra R. Kemp v. Colorado State University. US Supreme Court.

Sandra R. Kemp v. Virginia Department of Corrections (Warden, Virginia Correctional Center for Women)US Department of Justice.

Printed Sources

Letters and writings of contemporaries

Cocke, Bettie. "Letters from Napolean B. Drew of Mohemenco." (1893-1956).

Cocke, John Bowdoin. "Labor Contract with His Ex-Slaves." 1865.

Cocke, John Bowdoin. "Letter to John Hartwell Cocke of Bremo on ex-slaves leaving the plantation." 1865.

Cocke, John Bowdoin. "Letter to John Hartwell Cocke about one ex-slaves refusing to walk the mail from Belmead to Bremo after Slavery and Asking to Ride a Mule." 1865.

Cocke, John Hartwell. *Tobacco, the Bane of Virginia Husbandry.* 1860.

Cocke, John Hartwell. "Letter Mentions Tom Drew, Hostler, a Member of the Local Temperance Society, Returning to the Use of Alcohol."

Cocke, John Hartwell II. Journal 1853–1854: May 26, 1854. Shields Deposit.

Cocke, John Hartwell. "Letter (draft) to Gerrit Smith." December 13, 1839. Shields Deposit.

Cocke, Sally Elizabeth Bowdoin, Mrs. Phillip St. George Cocke. "Letter to John Hartwell Cocke about Ex-Slaves Leaving the Plantation." 1865.

Creasy, Archer (ex-slave). "Letter to John Hartwell." 1866.

Freedmen's Bureau. "Letter from the Provost Marshall in Gordonsville, Virginia to John Hartwell Cocke." 1866.

Guarino, Philip A. Colorado State University's Reference Letter for Sandra R. (Morris) Kemp. 1982.

Humphrey, Hubert H. "Letter to Sandra Morris." 1967.

"Letter from Mohemenco (writer unknown) to Ruby Mayo-Farris Weaver of Pennsylvania." August 6, 1927.

Morris, Annie Jane Bell. "Letter from Annie Morris of Mohemenco to son, Ivory Morris." New York City, NY. September 8, 1937.

Simms, Reverend William et al. of Mohemenco. "Letter to the Virginia State Board of Education." February 17, 1937.

Smith, Gerrit. "Letter to John Hartwell Cocke." December 11, 1840. Cocke Deposit.

"Undated, untitled draft of a letter to Gerrit Smith." Cocke Deposit.

Documents

American Colonization Society (ACS). "Roll of Emigrants that have been sent to the Colony of Liberia, Western Africa by the ACS and it auxiliaries to September 1843."

American Colonization Society. "Emigrants by Ship *Mariposa, Shute* sailed from Norfolk. June 1, 1842."

American Colonization Society. "Records: ACS, Series VI, Volume 15, Reel 314 (no page)."

Bell Family Reunion and Bell Pavilion Committees. "Minutes July 2014 and 2016 (Powhatan, Virginia)."

Belmead Post-Reconstruction Farm Book. "List of Employees of John Bowdoin Cocke." 1865 to 1889.

Carrington Family Reunion Committee. "Minutes August 2013 (Charlottesville, Virginia) and August 2014 (Powhatan, Virginia)."

James River District Baptist Association. "Minutes of the 49th Annual Session of the James River District Baptist Association Held with the Greenbrier Baptist Church, Powhatan County, Virginia." July 18 and 19, 1934.

Powhatan Combined Organization Committee. "Pocahontas Class Reunion 1937–1972 Program." February 12, 1995. Powhatan, Virginia.

Pocahontas Elementary School. "Certificate of Promotion. 1959–1960."

Powhatan Elementary School. "Elementary School Report, Powhatan County Public Schools." 1967–1968.

Pocahontas High School. "Certificates of Honor." 1960–1961 and 1962–1963.

The Powhatan County Branch of the National Association for the Advancement of Colored People. "Pioneer Student Award." October 13, 2002.

Powhatan County Board of Supervisors and School Board. "Minutes, July 24, 1954."

Progressive Negro Citizens. "Demands for Equal Opportunities to Powhatan Board of Supervisors." 1963.

Work Progress Administration of Virginia. "Historical Inventory." 1936–1937.

Newspapers

Current Comments. Cooperative Extension Service/Colorado State University
Charleston Gazette-Mail
Kiowa County Press
Mission Magazine
Millinery Information Bureau
Powhatan Today
Richmond Times-Dispatch

Rocky Mountain News
Sew News
Sew Business
The Goochland Gazette
The Washington Post

Periodicals

Belmeadian Newsletter. St. Emma Military Academy, Rock Castle, Virginia (Powhatan, Virginia), April 1960.

Big Chief. Powhatan County Public Schools. Powhatan, Virginia, 1965.

The Sabre. St. Emma Military Academy, Rock Castle, Virginia (Powhatan, Virginia), 1965.

Secondary Works

Biographies
Encyclopedia Virginia

- May 10, 2017. http://www.encyclopediavirginia.org/cocke_john_hartwell_1780-1866
- May 10, 2017. http://www.encyclopediavirginia.org/cocke_philip_st_george_1809-1861.

Powhatan County Historical Society

- Accessed October 8, 2012. http://www.powhatanhistoricalsociety.org/cemetry/j-morris-bio2.htm1.
- "James Morris Biography." Cemetery Index. Sandra Morris Kemp. Powhatan, Virginia, 2008.
- Oral History Committee. "Oral History of Ivory Emmett Morris." Jane Hewins. Powhatan, Virginia, 1999.

Francis Emma Inc. (Belmead) Historical and Cultural Committee

- "From Cocke's Belmead Plantation to Freedom: An African American Family's Documented Sojourn," Sandra Morris Kemp, Powhatan, Virginia, (2004).

Wikipedia

- "American Antislavery Society." Accessed November 8, 2017. https://en.wikipedia.org/wiki/American_Antislavery_Society.
- "American Colonization Society." Accessed November 8, 2017. https://en.wikipedia.org/wiki/American_Colonization_Society.
- "Belmead (Powhatan, Virginia)." Accessed November 7, 2017. https://en.wikipedia.org/wiki/Belmead_Powhatan_Virginia.
- "Bremo Historical District." Accessed November 8, 2017. https://en.wikipedia.org/wiki/Bremo_Historical_District.
- "Four-Mile Tree." Accessed November 8, 2017. https://en.wikipedia.org/wiki/Four_Mile_Tree.
- "Gerrit Smith." Accessed November 7, 2017. https://en.wikipedia.org/wiki/Gerrit_Smith.
- "John Brown (Abolitionist)." Accessed November 8, 2017. https://en.wikipedia.org/wiki/John_Browne_Abolitionist.
- "John Hartwell Cocke." Accessed September 4, 2017. https://en.wikipedia.org/wiki/John_Hartwell_Cocke.
- "Mount Pleasant Plantation." Accessed September 4, 2017. https://en.wikipedia.org/wiki/Mount_Pleasant_Plantation.
- "Philip St. George Cocke." Accessed September 4, 2017. https://en.wikipedia.org/wiki/Philip_St._George_Cocke.
- "Richard Cocke." Accessed September 4, 2017. https://en.wikipedia.org/wiki/Richard_Cocke.

Other Books

African American Religious History: A Documentary Witness (Thomas Wentworth Higgenson: "Slave Songs and Spirituals"). Edited by Milton C. Servett. Durham: Duke University Press, 1985.

Burke, Julian F. IV. *Lest We Forget: A Tribute to My Ancestors*. Charlottesville, Virginia, 2000.

Cocke, Philip St. George. *Plantation and Farm Instruction Records*. Virginia Historical Society, 1854.

Couture, Richard T. *Powhatan: A Bicentennial History*. Richmond, Virginia: The Dietz Press, 1980.

Dear Master: Letters of a Slave Family. Edited by Randall M. Miller. The University of Georgia Press, 1990.

Hudgins, Dennis. *Surry County, Virginia, Register of Free Negroes*. Virginia Genealogical Society, 1995.

Kemp, Sandra R. Morris. *Black History in Powhatan County, Virginia*. Powhatan, Virginia, 2005.

Kemp, Sandra. *Hat Making Made Simple*. Denver, Colorado: Word Works, 1987.

Kiowa County. Compiled by Roleta D. Teal and Betty Lee Jacobs. Kiowa County: Colorado Bicentennial Committee, 1976.

Powhatan County Heritage Book Committee. *Powhatan County Heritage Book 1776 to 2008: A Historical Review of Powhatan County and Its People*. Walsworth Publishing Company, 2010.

Renehan, Edward J. Jr. *The Secret Six: The True Tale of the Men Who Conspired with John Brown*. The University of South Carolina Press, 1997.

Whitt, R. Michael. *"Free Indeed!" The Trials and Triumphs of Enslaved and Freedmen in Antebellum Virginia*. Virginia Baptist Historical Society, Center for Baptist Heritage and Studies: University of Richmond, 2011.

Articles

"Arts and Fashion." *Richmond Magazine* (2017): 17.

The Associate Press. "Trump Tells Colleges to Back Free Speech or Risk Losing Money." *The Richmond Times Dispatch* (Friday, March 22, 2019): B5.

Bendel, Peggy. "Resources for Custom Decorated Hats." *Sew News* (1988).

Brown, Deneen L. "Va. to Mark 400 Years Since Arrival of Enslaved Africans." *The Washington Post*, (Sunday, August 26, 2018), A14.

Bush, Casey. "New Ways with Soft Hats for Fall." *Casey Associates/ Millinery Information Bureau* (August 1992).

Cooks, Carlos. "Ira Kemp-Founder of the Harlem Labor Union," Carlos Cooks and Black Nationalism from Garvey to Malcolm. *The Majority Press* (1992): 51–53. http://books.google.com/books?id=ggPc8Ejn3QEC&source=gbs.navlinkss

Copley, Michael. "History, Lessons." *Powhatan Today* (August 20, 2008).

Costa, Thomas. "Search the Runaway Slave Database, Virginia Runaways: Runaway Slave Advertisements from 18th Century Virginia Newspapers." University of Virginia's College at Wise. http://jefferson.village.virginia.edu:8090/xslt/servlet/ramunujan. XSLTServlet?xml=vcdh/xml

"Cox Family Story: General Cox." Ancient Faces.Com. Accessed August 10, 2005. http://www.ancientfaces.com/research/story/383053.

Daniels, Paul. "New Extension Agent Assumes Duties Here." *Kiowa County Press* (August 25, 1982). www.kiowacountypress.net.

Darrell, Emily. "Former Students Look Back on Struggle to Integrate Schools." *Powhatan Today* (February 26, 2013).

Elder, Darrell, "Mohemenco Historical Marker Dedicated." *Powhatan Today* (October 10, 2007).

Elder, Darrell. "A Hidden Slice of Powhatan's African American History." *Powhatan Today* XX no. 7 (February 15, 2006): 1A and 3A.

Elder, Darrell. "Stepping Back 40 Years." *Powhatan Today* XX, no. 8 (February 22, 2006): 1A and 3A.

"Embroidery News." *Topix* (2017). Accessed June 1, 2017. http://www.topix.com/hobbies/embroidery
http://www.topix.com/city/powhatan

"The Geography of Slavery." *Virginia Gazette* or *American Advertiser* (Hayes), December 4, 1784. Accessed September 6, 2006. http://etext.lib.virginia.edu/etcbin/ot2.www-costa?specfil=/web/data/users/costa/costa.o2w&.

Hat Making Made Simple: The Milliner. Book review. *Sew Business* (June 1989).

Jarvis, Jake. "Fade Away: Not Yet-Barber Marks 70th Birthday at Shop." *Charleston Gazette-Mail* (June 1, 2015).

Kemp, Sandra. "The Trades Tradition: From Miller to Milliner." *Powhatan County Heritage Book 1777-2009: A Historical Review of Powhatan County and Its People* (2010): 96–97.

Kemp, Sandra. "Sewing for the Home and Conserving Energy While Sewing." *Current Comments* (Cooperative Extension Service/Colorado State University Newsletter, November 1984).

Kemp, Sandra. "Carrington Descendants Reunite." *Powhatan Today* XXVII, no. 36 (September 10, 2014): 1A, 7A.

McCartney, Martha W. "The Historical Background of the Mount Pleasant-Swann's Point Tract, Surry County, Virginia." Accessed December 3, 2005. http://www.mountpleasantrestoration.com/html/resear/mcc/hist-14.html.

McCartney, Martha W. "The Historical Background of the Mount Pleasant-Swann's Point Tract, Surry County, Virginia." Accessed December 3, 2005. http://www.mountpleasantrestoration.com/html/resear/mcc/hist-15.html.

McFarland, Laura. "Sandra Kemp Garments on Display at the Valentine." *Powhatan Today* XXX, no. 21 (May 24, 2017).

Newman-Stanley, Bonnie. "Fall Hats on Display Downtown." *Richmond Times Dispatch.* Tuesday, September 15, 1992: 2C.

The Mount Pleasant Foundation. "Historical Background of Mount Pleasant." Accessed October 29, 2015. http://mountpleasant-plantation.com?page_id=114.

The Mount Pleasant Foundation. "Journey into the Past-Mount Pleasant Plantation." Spring Grove, Virginia. Accessed November 7, 2017. http://mountpleasantplantation.com.

The Mount Pleasant Foundation, "Mount Pleasant Plantation-Nicholas and Sally Cocke Faulcon." Accessed October 29, 2015. http://mountpleasantplantation.com?page_id=151.

Newton, Karen. "A New Fashion Exhibit at the Valentine Takes a Glimpse at Richmond's Most Notable Art Patrons." *Style Weekly* (May 2, 2017): 1–2. Accessed May 24, 2017. http://www.styleweekly.com.richmond/a-new-fashion-exhibit-at-the-valentine-takes-a-gli.http://www.richmond.com/news/local/powhatan-today/sandra-k

Potter, Bill. "Africans Arrive at Jamestown." August 20, 1619. Accessed September 21, 2017. https://landmarkevents.org/africans-arrive-at-jamestown-1619.

"Powhatan Leadership Institute graduates Its Newest 'Farm Team.'" *Powhatan Today* (April 30, 2008): 8A.

Rocky Mountain News Staff. "Appeals Court Rules Against Ex-CSU Agent." *Rocky Mountain News* (Friday, November 3, 1989).

Ryan, Roslyn. "Recovered Ferry Will Be on Display During Event: Craft, Submerged in James, Helped Make River Crossing Convenient." *The Goochland Gazette* 63, no. 21 (May 31, 2018): 1, 3.

Sisters of the Blessed Sacrament. "History, Healing, Hope." *Mission Magazine* LXXIV, no. 1 (June 28, 2008): 2–5.

"Slavery in America: Virginia Slave Law Summary and Record." Accessed March 10, 2006. http://www.slaveryinamerica.org/geography/slave_laws_Virginia.htm.

Trott, Jon. "A Very Incomplete History on Black/White Romance in America." *Cornerstone Magazine* 26, no. 111 (1997): 7–9. Accessed April 14, 2004. http://www.cornerstonemag.com/features/iss111/history.htm.

"Virginia Slaves Freed in Virginia after 1782." http://www.freeafricanamericans.com/virginiafreeafter1782.htm.

Theses and Dissertations

Coyner, Martin Boyd Jr. "John Hartwell Cocke of Bremo: Agriculture and Slavery in the Ante-Bellum South." Doctoral dissertation. University of Virginia, 1961.

ABOUT THE AUTHOR

Sandra Rose Morris Kemp, local historian, lived her early years in Mohemenco Hamlet, Powhatan, Virginia. Upon reaching adulthood, she lived in Washington, DC; Greenbelt, Maryland; Eads, Colorado; and Aurora, Colorado. Since 1988, she has resided in the metropolitan Richmond, Virginia, area with her husband, Darryl Kemp. They have a daughter and two grandsons living in the area.

Ms. Kemp's *education* includes attendance at Pocahontas Elementary School and Pocahontas and Powhatan High Schools. She pursued higher education at West Virginia State College, Howard University, Virginia Commonwealth University (BFA in fashion design, 1971), the University of the District of Columbia (MA in adult education, 1977), and the University of Maryland (advanced graduate specialist in adult, extension, and continuing education, 1988). Ms. Kemp's *other training* includes the following: Leadership for Innovation and Change (NOVA University–Fort Lauderdale),

US Peace Corps, US Army National Guard, Powhatan Leadership Institute, Richmond Hill Pastoral Care and Counseling, and Foundations for BeFriender Ministry (University of St. Thomas–Minnesota [the St. Paul Seminary School of Divinity]).

Her *work experience* includes teaching in correctional education, cooperative extension service, and public housing. She wrote the book *Hat Making Made Simple*, developed the curriculum for the Milliner Correspondence Course, and taught millinery. She has also worked in the field of retail management.

Ms. Kemp became the first African American to graduate from Powhatan County High School and Virginia Commonwealth University Fashion Design Department and to serve as a Colorado State University Extension agent in Southeast Colorado.

She has served on the following *boards and committees*: Francis Emma Inc. (board of directors, co-facilitator for the Belmead Granary Planning Circle and Oral History Project), War Memorial Building Use Committee, Tourism Board, Social Services Board, Chamber of Commerce Pictorial History Committee, 150th Anniversary of the Civil War County Committee, and Pocahontas Middle School Revitalization Use Committee.

Ms. Kemp's *interests and hobbies* include the following: property rental, home decorating, millinery and fashion design, historical preservation, research and writing, health and fitness, relaxing with jazz music, watching documentary programs, photography, and traveling.

CPSIA information can be obtained
at www.ICGtesting.com
Printed in the USA
LVHW072207151020
668965LV00023B/2514

9 781098 021887